TRAVELERS
ALONG
THE WAY

THE MEN AND WOMEN WHO SHAPED MY LIFE

BENEDICT J.
GROESCHEL
C.F.R.

SERVANT
BOOKS

PUBLISHED BY ST. ANTHONY MESSENGER PRESS
CINCINNATI, OHIO

Unless otherwise noted, Scripture passages have been taken from the *Revised Standard Version*, Catholic edition. Copyright 1946, 1952, 1971 by the Division of Christian Education of the National Council of Churches of Christ in the USA. Used by permission. All rights reserved.

Cover and book design by Mark Sullivan
Cover photo courtesy of Eternal Word Television Network

LIBRARY OF CONGRESS CATALOGING-IN-PUBLICATION DATA
Groeschel, Benedict J.
Travelers along the way : the men and women who shaped my life /
Benedict J. Groeschel.
p. cm.
Includes bibliographical references (p.   ) and index.
ISBN 978-0-86716-984-3 (pbk. : alk. paper) 1. Groeschel, Benedict J. 2. Groeschel, Benedict J.—Friends and associates. 3. Catholic Church—United States—Clergy—Biography. I. Title.
BX4705.G62293A3 2010
282.092—dc22
[B]
2010034394

ISBN 978-0-86716-984-3

Copyright ©2010, Benedict J. Groeschel. All rights reserved.

Published by Servant Books, an imprint of St. Anthony Messenger Press.
28 W. Liberty St.
Cincinnati, OH 45202
www.AmericanCatholic.org
www.ServantBooks.org

Printed in the United States of America.

Printed on acid-free paper.

10 11 12 13 14 5 4 3 2 1

TRAVELERS ALONG THE WAY

To all the many travelers I have encountered
along the road,
both living and deceased.

CONTENTS

The Journey Through Life

For the believer life is a journey, a road laid out for us by the providence of God and guided by the divine law and the teaching of Christ. Human life can be considered the intersection of our personal thoughts and deeds with the mysterious workings of Divine Providence. Together these two elements form our existence.

Our lives move from small, seemingly insignificant occasions, which we quickly forget, all the way up to events that burn themselves deeply into our memories. Sometimes we confront troubles and even catastrophes—things that alter us forever and seem to put an end to all that has come before for us. Yet somehow or other we go on—even when that seems impossible. We slowly incorporate even difficulties and catastrophes into the whole that we call our lives, permitting them to play their part in forming us into the people we are constantly becoming.

Of course, as a person grows older, particularly when the end of life is apparently not very far off, the past takes on special significance. One is drawn at such a time to recollection, to revisiting people who are long gone. One tries over and over again to make sense of what has happened during one's life. It goes without saying that those who have faith and trust will have much to use as their guide when looking back, when recalling the people and events that have shaped their lives.

I find it impossible to understand a person who simply moves from one event to another without any kind of purpose, goal, or light to guide their human existence. Our lives and the lives of others have great meaning; they are not random meanderings. Providence and faith lead us on.

As we make our life's journey, we meet others who are doing the same—fellow travelers.

We first encounter them when we are very small children, for it is then that we become aware of others as real people: our parents and siblings and other family members affect us in ways that are incalculable. They remain forever a part of us, even if they fail us. We cannot ever dissolve the connection to them completely. Later we meet others who become profound influences in our lives. With them we may develop relationships of love or hurt or dislike. Public figures whom we might not have actually met can still have a great impact on us, affecting us deeply for good or for ill.

This book is about such people, the ones whom I have encountered along my life's way.

I must make it very clear that in no way am I trying to include all those who have been significant in my life. That would be an impossible task, and I suspect no one would read such a book, even those who are part of my life's journey. This book is instead comprised of a series of vignettes of some of those whom I have known who have changed my life, sometimes greatly, sometimes in little ways

The significance of others on one's life often can never be fully expressed but only suggested. Human relationships are mysterious; sometimes the most important things about them are impossible to convey with mere words. So I have decided to make this book a series of glimpses. I want to take a look—a glance really—at the lives of interesting and often colorful people who have shaped my life by their ideas or their behavior. I hope and I expect that these people will have something to teach my readers as well.

I Am You

Some years ago a very fine Jesuit from Fordham University, Fr. Joseph Fitzpatrick, S.J., who worked all his life with the Latino people of New York City as a sociologist, was greatly delighted when he was elected "Puerto Rican of the Year." At a gathering toward the end of his career, which was held to honor him, he said, "I am you. You have made me who I am." It was not an entirely accurate statement, but it was a startling one. Indeed, a good number of the people in the room that day had been very significant in his life, and he realized—humbly and gratefully—that they had been instrumental in helping him become the person that he was. This is something for all of us to think about. We are in so many respects the people we have met and known along the way. Sometimes this is a blessing and sometimes…perhaps not. We ought to intend always to do the best we can with the many influences that come into our lives so that we can receive from others those things that will enable us to make the best of the short journey that we call earthly life.

This book includes a number of people who have been very significant in different ways. Some are famous. Some are known for their holiness, like Mother Teresa and Cardinal Cooke. Others come from very different backgrounds, from a devout Presbyterian minister to an old Jewish man who ran a dry-cleaning business. Some are people that you have probably never heard of. Others have names that are known to all.

Some of them are people with secure places in history. Others will be quickly forgotten by all but their friends and relatives.

I will try to give you snapshots of some of my fellow travelers, the ones who have made a great difference in my life. I do this because I hope to draw you into thinking and meditating on what others have done for you, on how your life has been enriched and deepened by those you have met along the way. It is my hope that this book will help you recognize the blessings that others have brought into your life. Perhaps it will help some of you to better understand and even forgive the human faults and failings of those who have hurt you. I hope that we will all become more grateful for and sensitive to what we have gained from the fellow travelers we have met along life's way.

A Question of Choice

In order to make the selection of which fellow travelers to include in this book, I consciously chose to omit all relatives, although (in my humble opinion) some are very interesting. I also left out many people who profoundly affected me for the best on my journey to God. This group included numerous priests, sisters, and brothers who led me through three decades of education. I have been very blessed in many ways; one of them is that most of my education was accomplished by devout teachers. I could have written many chapters on such people. My memories of Sr. Victoria and Mother Dolorita are numerous and clear. Both would have made excellent additions to this book. These wonderful Dominicans were very important in my early formation, as was Sr. Mercedita who passed away recently, well into her nineties. These sisters taught their subjects well, and they also showed by example what the Christian life ought to be. I feel the same way about many of the Sisters of Charity and the Sisters of St. Joseph whom I knew during the early part of my life. Although I cannot include them all in this little volume of reminiscences, I have chosen to begin this book with a story about one of the sisters who greatly affected me. She was a wonderful Sister of Charity who has much to teach us all and whose influence is still strong in my life.

CHAPTER ONE

Sr. Teresa Maria

I was blessed in my early education. I went to schools taught by a wonderful group of people: Catholic nuns. These were the old-fashioned kind of sisters, the ones who so capably ran schools throughout the country in the days prior to the Second Vatican Council and shortly thereafter. There were huge congregations of sisters back then, and all of them could be easily identified by their distinctive religious habits. Almost every parish had a convent in which such sisters lived, and they all lived according to very serious rules of common life: prayer, silence, no personal ownership.

Everyone who went to Catholic schools in those days has a story or two about the sisters—particularly the ones who were too strict or a little grouchy. I have some such stories of my own, but for the most part, thinking back on the sisters who were my teachers for so many years brings me happiness and a profound sense of gratitude.

One of the greatest people I ever knew was a tiny little Sister of Charity from Convent Station, New Jersey, who taught in Our Lady of Victory School in Jersey City, Sr. Teresa Maria. But this sister did not simply teach; she brought joy and peace and kindliness to everyone in the class. I was told by older sisters in her community that she had spent about forty-five years teaching the second grade. As if that's not enough, she also spent a number of years teaching first graders. Sr. Teresa Maria never got excited. She never was cross. She smiled at us all, and we loved her.

As my year in second grade progressed, however, I gradually became aware of something very strange about Sr. Teresa Maria, something that sparked my curiosity. Every day after school she came out of the convent, and she was always carrying something. It was usually a box, although sometimes it was a tray covered with a large white napkin. She then walked down a rather run-down street called Westside Avenue, until she came to what we used to call a tenement house, into which she mysteriously disappeared.

I became more and more intrigued as the days passed, imagining all sorts of reasons for these trips. Finally one day I decided I had to know what was going on, and I followed her at a distance. Careful to remain unobserved and proud of my detective ability, I was certain I was on the verge of discovering what Sister's secret visits were all about—until she disappeared through the door of the tenement building. At that point I stopped dead, not sure how to proceed.

After a few minutes however, I began to form a new plan. On the street level of this building was a barber named Giuseppe. (In those days—at least as far as I was concerned—all barbers were Italian.) I realized that Giuseppe and his barbershop could be crucial in helping me solve the mystery of Sister's comings and goings, and so, armed with a dime (the price of a haircut back then), I entered the shop. Delighted to discover that the barber was every bit as talkative as I had hoped, I climbed into his chair.

As Giuseppe cut my hair, I interrogated him subtly (or at least I was trying to be subtle). Soon the old barber spilled the beans. He told me that Sister came to take care of an elderly woman who lived on the top floor, a woman who was very ill. This was excellent information, but like all great detectives, I craved firsthand knowledge.

After my haircut I went around the building and climbed up the rickety old porch that served as a fire escape. When I finally I made it to the top floor, I still wasn't sure what I would see, but what I actually saw came as a great shock.

At that time I had seen only one movie in my life, Walt Disney's animated version of *Snow White and the Seven Dwarfs,* something my dad had taken me to when I was in the first grade. In those days before television, I thought the figures in the movie—we still called them "moving pictures"— were quite real. As you may remember, one of the characters in this film was a wicked old witch who threatened the life of Snow White. I peered through the window into a dark apartment, looking for Sister, but I didn't see her. Instead, staring directly at me, only a few inches back from the window, was the wicked witch—exactly as she had appeared in the movie!

My breath caught in my throat as our eyes met for the briefest of instants. Then I was in rapid motion, jumping off the milk box on which I had perched and running as fast as I was able. I remember knocking over empty beer bottles and a few potted tomato plants as I scrambled down the stairs, but I didn't care. I had to get out of there as quickly as my legs would carry me.

I kept on going, not stopping until I reached the church. There, completely out of breath, I dropped to my knees at the shrine of the Blessed Virgin. She looked sweetly down at me— as she still does these many decades later. I prayed with an intensity inspired by fear, because I had just encountered a witch.

Eventually a question came into my mind: Why didn't the witch hurt Sr. Teresa? The answer came soon after the question: because Sister was kind to the witch—she was actually kind to a witch! Maybe if people were kinder to witches, I thought, they wouldn't be so bad. As I was contemplating these thoughts, words that I had never heard before came very clearly into my mind: "Become a priest."

I didn't want to be a priest. My career had already been decided. I was sure I was destined to be a fireman.

Not too far from our home was the firehouse, with its gleaming red fire engines. The firemen were always kind to kids, giving us candy and nuts. We often waited around, hoping there would be an alarm so that we could watch the firemen come sliding down the pole they used instead of stairs. I admired them. I wanted to be like them and to do all the exciting things they did. As far as I was concerned, my vocation was already decided

My walk home took me past the rectory, which looked rather forbidding. Fortunately the pastor, Fr. Tom O'Donnell, was a delightful old Irishman who walked through the entire parish every day, greeting everyone. As I looked at the rectory, I realized that I couldn't avoid it completely. I had to at least think about becoming a priest. But I didn't tell a soul.

The following year I entered the third grade and a different school. I would no longer see Sr. Teresa Maria every day. Sr. Consolata, a Dominican, all in white except for her black veil, taught my class. One day she gave me a small gift, a holy card, and on it she wrote the words, "*Ora pro me.*" When I showed it to my father, he asked me to find out why her inscription was in Latin. I asked her, and she looked me straight in the eye and said, "Because you're going to be a priest." This made me very uncomfortable. My cover had somehow been blown, and I was in grave danger of losing my identity as a fireman-to-be.

I still discussed this with almost no one, but by the fifth or sixth grade, in some way it had become very obvious to me and others that the priesthood was to be my destiny, and so it has been. But for the beginnings of my vocation, I always go back to that day when I surreptitiously followed a wonderful, kindly nun as she carried food to a "wicked witch."

Many years later, Sr. Teresa was present at my first Mass, and I recounted this story in my sermon. Some of the other sisters then told me that the old woman whom Sr. Teresa so faithfully cared for was very anti-Catholic and really quite unpleasant. Yet Sister cared for her for seven years because the old woman had no one else. The poor old soul could never even get herself to call her helper "Sister."

How important are the people we meet as we make our way through life—especially those who have a vital message for us. Sr. Teresa had no idea that she was giving a message to anyone. This was not her intention, but her work of charity, of kindness, her holy way of doing things, her saintliness, all had an effect on me that continues to this day. For seventy years it has been clear to me that one of the first travelers I met as I was just beginning my journey was, in fact, a quiet saint.

CHAPTER TWO

Mr. Graff

I grew up in the New York metropolitan area, and as far as I was concerned, Catholics and Jews composed most of the Caucasian world. For me at the time, Protestants were generally African-Americans, people who seemed to approach their religious lives with an extraordinary enthusiasm and fervent prayer. These people, whom I loved, seemed to live in a different world, one I might occasionally visit but never inhabit.

Among Catholics and Jews, however, I was totally at home. The two groups lived their entire lives in the same neighborhoods, at times squabbling but usually getting along quite well. We were, in fact, very much parts of each other's lives. Even if you went to Catholic school, as I did, you were very aware of the Jewish holidays. We all knew that on Rosh Hashanah and Yom Kippur, there would be almost no one in the public schools. All our Jewish friends would spend the entire day in the synagogue with their families.

Among our neighbors were older Jewish men and women who were still Orthodox. Nothing interfered with their observance of the Sabbath (they called it *"Shabbos"*); without exception, this one day of the week was given over to rest and to God. I have many memories of them observing the long hours of the Sabbath very devoutly.

One of these people was Mr. Graff. He ran a dry-cleaning business with the somewhat poetic name of "The French Dry Cleaners," although after all these years I still haven't figured out what was French about the place. With his spectacles perched on the end of his nose, Mr. Graff could be found day after day fixing pants and expertly sewing things.

You must understand that Mr. Graff was not just an ordinary dry cleaner; he was a philosopher. Not only would he hold forth on any one of a variety of subjects, but he was willing to discuss them in detail with a thirteen- or fourteen-year-old boy, something most adults would never do. I have to say that, despite the very fine priests who were in our parish, Mr. Graff ended up being my spiritual director.

Seemingly conversant in all subjects, Mr. Graff had an endless reservoir of facts and figures in his head, and standing by his counter, I learned a lot of things. He was a keen observer of human life and was always eager to share his thoughts about politics, most of the practitioners of which he did not like at all. For a long time I listened to his every word, taking each one to heart. I'm sure I didn't realize it then, but I was being regularly exposed to a kind of simple and kindly wisdom, something that has become rare in our world.

After several years of listening and learning, the day came to say good-bye to Mr. Graff. I walked into the French Dry Cleaners as I had done so many times before, but this time I was wearing a black suit. It was an old suit that Fr. Beggins, a young priest in our parish, had given to me. Mr. Graff had cut it down so that it would fit me, and it did fit—perfectly.

My life was about to change dramatically, change in ways I couldn't even imagine, but I certainly knew I had reached a turning point. I was on my way to the novitiate. In those days we were all expected to show up in a black suit with a white shirt and a black tie—the unvarying uniform of the seminarian.

Mr. Graff looked me up and down as I stood there in my black suit. Finally, he said to me in the accent that once had seemed very pronounced but which I now hardly noticed, "Look, I don't understand about monasteries, but I'll give you a piece of advice: Be a good boy."

It was a great piece of advice.

His beloved wife of sixty years then came into the shop. As older people of so many nationalities do, the Graffs seemed to communicate with each other best by shouting. It was a strange way of being affectionate, one that I didn't quite understand, but I had gotten used to it with older immigrants. The ensuing dialogue went more or less like this:

Mr. Graff (in a voice that could be heard blocks away): "Ain't you gonna say good-bye to Pete [which was my name]?"

Mrs. Graff: "So...where's he going?"

Mr. Graff: "By the monastery."

Mrs. Graff (sounding shocked and disturbed): "By the monastery? That's terrible. He's just a kid. How could he go by the monastery? He's too little."

Mr. Graff: "You never heard of freedom of religion? Separation of church and state? What do you want me to do, knock him down on the floor and sit on him? He wants to go by the monastery."

Mrs. Graff: "Shut up! You should take a little walk and explain to him about the bees and the birds."

At that moment I realized it was time to say good-bye to both of them, and I did. I didn't even suspect it then, but I would never see them again. It was ten years later and after I was ordained that I got my first home visit. By that time both of them had died.

But I remember this good man and his wife, who were genuinely concerned about me and were dealing with something quite beyond the things with which they were familiar. Over the years I have often envisioned old Mr. Graff looking at me over the battlements of eternity, just as he looked at me over the counter in his store when he said to me, "Be a good boy." This, by the way, is advice I've always tried to follow.

CHAPTER THREE

Br. Ferdinando

At the age of seventeen I arrived in my black suit at St. Felix Friary in Huntington, Indiana. My goal was to become a Capuchin-Franciscan friar. However, I had a strong suspicion I was getting off on the wrong foot as soon as the door opened. Instead of acting holy and solemn, as I had planned, I started grinning broadly. I couldn't help it, you see, because the door was opened by an elf.

Dressed in the brown Capuchin habit, the person who greeted me was very short and quite fat; his arms and legs were stubby, and he had what can best be described as a natural tonsure. He introduced himself to me, in a voice that was nearly a falsetto, as Br. Ferdinando Piconi—which I later learned means "pine cone" in Italian. With a musical Italian accent, he told me he was delighted that I came from New York, because he had lived in New York for a number of years after departing from Sicily.

Then Br. Ferdinando instructed me to pray for him every day in order that he might have a happy death. As a youngster I thought this a bit odd—especially after an acquaintance of only a few seconds—but I agreed. And every day for months, whenever I would pass him in the silence of the cloister, he would whisper, "Don't forget. Remember to pray for a happy death for me." I assumed he thought I was the forgetful type.

Time passed quickly, and soon it was the Vigil of All Saints Day—what the world calls Halloween. We were having breakfast in silence, as was the custom. It was after Mass in the early hours of the morning. Suddenly Br. Ferdinando—who had looked fine up to that moment—landed hard on the floor. Obviously he had had a serious heart attack or something similar, and things didn't look good.

We carried him up the stairs, telling one another, "Get the doctor! Get the doctor!" Br. Ferdinando, however, who seemed to have a better grasp of what was going on than the rest of us did, kept calling out in his high-pitched voice, "Get the priest! Get the priest!"

It happens sometimes in human events that someone is very appropriately chosen to have one and only one great moment in life. And this seemed to be the moment for the priest who said the prayers for the dying for Br. Ferdinando. His voice sounded like gravel rubbing against the side of a casket that is being lowered into the ground. As a teenager, kneeling there attempting to pray, it became clear to me that this man had been born for the prayers for the dying. All the young brothers were kneeling around Br. Ferdinando's little cot in his cell. The tiny room couldn't accommodate us all, and many of us found ourselves out in the hallway as the priest began. He prayed in rumbling Latin, changing into English only to intone, "Depart, O Christian soul." As he spoke, it dawned on me that if Br. Ferdinando wasn't actually dying, this priest and these words might actually push him over the edge.

We were all still fervently praying when we heard the ambulance approaching through the fields. We didn't move, of course, but continued our prayers.

Then we heard the sound of people running, and the ambulance attendants arrived—breathless—at the door to

Br. Ferdinando's cell, just in time to see him open his eyes, wave weakly at us all, and say, "*Arrivaderci.*" Br. Ferdinando did leave in the ambulance. He went, however, not to the hospital but to the funeral parlor.

He didn't have any family in America, and so the funeral Mass, which was celebrated at 7:00 in the morning, was attended by many of the German-American farmers who populated that part of Indiana. They turned out to be the perfect people to invite to a funeral. They never moved. In fact, some of them looked as if they were painted on the back of the pew.

At the end of the Mass, these devout laypeople processed out of the chapel, led by the cross bearer and acolytes and followed by the young brothers, who numbered about thirty. Then came the few priests and old brothers, carrying the casket. Behind them were the celebrant and the deacon—the Venerable Fr. Solanus Casey. The old priests and brothers, including Fr. Solanus, had great white beards and looked to me to be extraordinarily ancient.

I was assigned the role of doorman. It was my job to hold open the door that led to the cemetery while the procession passed through. I did so solemnly as the brother next to me rang the chapel bell. As this rather colorful procession went out and made its way up a small hill into the sunrise, my confrere looked at me and whispered, "A funeral by Cecil B. DeMille. He sure got a great death and funeral."

Perhaps, but that doesn't matter. Br. Ferdinando had received from God what he most wanted. He had prayed for a happy death, and he had been given one. Since then I've been following his example and praying for one for myself. I suggest you do the same.

CHAPTER FOUR

Fr. Solanus Casey

I consider two encounters to be among the greatest blessings I have ever received. One was with the Venerable Fr. Solanus Casey, an old Capuchin. The other was with Blessed Mother Teresa of Calcutta. It would be impossible for me to say which of these two people—who were very different from each other—was the greater. Each was truly and thoroughly holy. Each was extraordinarily close to God.

When I arrived at my novitiate—after meeting Br. Ferdinando—I soon had the opportunity to observe Fr. Solanus, the very gentle, holy soul whom many people already called a saint. This is because he was one of those few people who managed to achieve in their earthly lives the goal of full service to God without any complaint. This is also because many people claimed physical miracles had actually been performed through this humble man's prayers.

Actually, by the time of Fr. Solanus's death in 1967, there were nearly nine hundred claims that his prayers had been the cause of favors received from God, from small things to heal-ings of severe illnesses. I have met some people who could give examples of this. Br. Leo Wollenweber, who is vice-postulator of the cause of canonization of Fr. Solanus, tells me that over the years he has received about two thousand reports of favors short of miracles that people throughout the world ascribe to the prayers of this humble but great Capuchin friar.

A number of biographies of Fr. Solanus are easily available, and so there is no need to speak here in detail about the events of his life. However, there is one event that is recorded in some of those books about which I do want to tell. It is a story in which I participated.

As a young novice, I was unable to sleep one night. Finally I gave up trying, and at about two o'clock in the morning, I went down to the darkened chapel to pray. I assumed I would be alone, but it turned out that I was not.

As I turned on the two strong lights that were trained on the altar, I discovered Fr. Solanus in front of me, kneeling on the top step in front of the tabernacle. Seeing him was a shock, because he was clearly in some kind of ecstasy and completely unaware of my presence. He didn't even realize that I had turned on the lights. His eyes were fixed on the door of the tabernacle. The arms of this elderly man were extended outward in prayer, and as the seconds passed, I realized he was absolutely unmoving; his arms did not tremble in the slightest.

I watched for a few minutes, and during that time he did not move at all. I then put out the lights and went back to my room, feeling very embarrassed. It was as if I had seen something that I should not have, something that was intensely private. In fact, as I look back on that night, I now realize I was wrong. Those few moments gave me the opportunity to be a witness in Fr. Solanus's cause for beatification, to enable the world to know a little more of his deep sanctity.

But this is not the image of Fr. Solanus that I most want to share with you. I have chosen instead a story that is not in most of his biographies and is in some ways much more fascinating. It is certainly more lighthearted—although it definitely didn't seem that way at the time.

It was about four o'clock in the afternoon one day during my novitiate. I believe it was early fall and growing cool—perhaps it was early or mid-October. Suddenly the alarm bell sounded, summoning the novices to come as quickly as possible. We obediently ran down the stairs to discover an enormous swarm of bees in one of the trees outside.

The monastery was surrounded by acres of apple orchards, and to pollinate the trees we needed bees. We kept several hives, each of which was home to thousands of bees. I thought I had grown used to them, but I had certainly never seen the bees do anything like what they were doing at that moment: Thousands of them were swarming angrily, creating what seemed to be a huge, threatening, dark mass. It almost looked like one single creature rather than countless tiny ones.

As we were watching this in utter astonishment, we received our instructions—ones that tested obedience to the limit. We were to put on protective hats, gloves, and nets; then we were to go outside to determine exactly what the problem was with the bees, as such events could have one of several causes. As if this were not enough, we were then supposed to fix things and calm the bees down.

Yearning for Jersey City (where you never see bees), I covered every inch of exposed skin as thoroughly as I could. Then, in the company of some of the other novices, I went outside and walked toward the bees as slowly as was humanly possible. My heart was pounding, and I felt absolutely helpless—pretty much the way condemned murderers must feel as they are being marched to the gallows. I knew no particular prayers that implored God for deliverance from bees, but you can be sure that I was composing some in record time.

Apparently, as we novices were getting ready to confront the swarm, the novice master had sent for Fr. Solanus. He seemed to appear out of nowhere, wearing his habit, just as he always did, and not bothering with any protection at all. As he walked toward the swarm of very angry bees, he casually told us all to remain calm. This proved a very difficult thing to do, because as he spoke thousands of bees started to swarm around him. I immediately included Fr. Solanus in my newly composed prayers for deliverance from bees.

As the bees swarmed and the buzzing increased, Fr. Solanus spoke quietly to them, telling them to calm down. He spoke as if to a person. Then he approached one of the hives and opened it—as if this were the most natural thing in the world to do.

After a moment's inspection of the hive, Fr. Solanus explained that the problem would be easy to remedy. There must be two queens, he told us. Removing the extra queen would remove the problem. Peering into the hive, which seemed to be pulsating with agitated bees, he asked us for help in finding the extra queen. I demurred. By that time I was so frightened that I couldn't have found the *Queen Mary*.

Fr. Solanus reached down into the hive. His arm was now black with bees, and bees were tangled in his long, white beard. He barely seemed to notice as he rummaged around for a few seconds. Then, looking pleased, he brought up a white wormlike creature: the queen. Wrapping her carefully in his handkerchief, he put her in his pocket.

I watched all this, absolutely amazed, sure that the bees would now turn on him to protect the queen. But that never happened. The bees continued to swarm, but not one of them stung him.

Once the queen was safely in his pocket, Fr. Solanus reached into his sleeve, removing handfuls of bees. Then he produced his harmonica and began to play "Mother Machree" to calm the bees down. Somehow it worked: They became less and less agitated and started to enter the hive. In a relatively short time, the bees were at peace again.

The event was surreal, seemingly impossible, but I witnessed it. No one could have done what Fr. Solanus did, but it happened, and what's more, Fr. Solanus didn't think there was anything particularly special about it. Neither, strangely, did some of the other novices, which puzzles me to this day.

At other times in my life I have observed events that have seemed utterly mysterious and have been surprised to discover that many of the people around me seemed not to notice them. This shows how unaware we are of the mysterious and how little we appreciate the out-of-the-ordinary. It also shows that we can refuse to see what is plainly before our eyes if it is something beyond our expectations. We resist acknowledging things for which we have no categories, events that might force us to change our view of things.

Often, while observing the actions of Mother Teresa or even the kind and gentle actions of Cardinal Terence Cooke, I have been astonished at the matter-of-fact attitude of most people toward them. People could regularly observe them in the midst of doing things with extraordinary holiness—usually not spectacular things, but things filled with holiness nonetheless —and somehow remain totally unaware of this.

Other events took place that are similar to Fr. Solanus's conversation with the bees. Sick people came to the monastery in large numbers to visit him and to ask for his prayers for healing. On one occasion a boy was carried in on a stretcher, and only a couple of weeks later was able to stand on his own legs and come to Mass at the monastery. I believe this boy was not Catholic but Jewish.

There were also claims from many people that Fr. Solanus had told them of things that would happen in the future. One man told me that he had visited Fr. Solanus at the St. Bonaventure Monastery to discuss whether his mother should have a third cancer operation or not. The man loved his mother greatly and did not want to put her through more surgery if it would not really help her. Like so many, this man depended on Fr. Solanus to help him make the right decision. He was confident that this simple priest would provide him with the right answer.

Always understanding and kind, Fr. Solanus first asked the man when his mother was scheduled to enter the hospital. When the man said that it was to be the following Wednesday, Fr. Solanus closed his eyes for a few minutes and then looked up. Quietly but confidently he told the man that he would know what to do on Wednesday morning and that there was no need to worry. The man later told me that early on Wednesday morning, his mother went home to God peacefully.

There was a man named Jimmy who was what most people used to call a hobo. The friars, however, would never use such a word. For them Jimmy was "one of the poor lads." They gave him a little job that didn't involve much more than sweeping up the friary, but it was a job, and it came complete with a little room in the basement.

Things seemed to be going well for Jimmy, and I know he was happy to have a permanent place to live, decent food, and some work to do. Then one day Fr. Solanus walked up to him and out of the blue said, "Brother James, it is not good for man to be alone, and one of our dear sisters in the Third Order of St. Francis is a widow. She needs a good husband to help her on her farm."

Jimmy's jaw dropped, and so did the broom he was using to sweep the floor. Then Jimmy was gone. He packed his stuff and got as far from the monastery and that woman's farm as he could. He was not going to fool around with someone like Fr. Solanus, who could tell the future.

All I can say in summary is that the memories of this extraordinary man, all of which come from less than a year in my life, will always remain with me. I will always recall his obvious prayerfulness, his quietness, and his gentleness. I can say without qualification that his deep holiness has had a profound effect on my life. In meeting him, I firmly believe that I met a saint.

I hope and pray that as you make your journey through life, you will also come across at least one of God's truly holy people. I also pray that you will realize this, for true sanctity is not always apparent. Such an encounter changes you in certain ways, and this is the real reason that God sends such people into our lives, to give us a glimpse of what true holiness really is and to leave us different from the way we were before, more aware of the Divine Presence.

We tend to think of saints as being somehow spectacular, different from everyone else. They are, but often in such quiet and hidden ways that we run the risk of not noticing them. To many Fr. Solanus was just another Capuchin friar—to some, in fact, he was a rather undistinguished Capuchin friar—but the humble friar who knelt in ecstasy before the Blessed Sacrament and who spoke to bees was far more than he appeared to be, far closer to God than those around him might have thought.

During the life of our Lord Jesus Christ, some people fell to their knees when they witnessed His miracles, His signs and wonders, His great works. Others, however, somehow managed to ignore Him, while still others plotted His murder. It is important for all of us to make a very serious attempt to see what is before our eyes, to notice that sometimes the will of God is being made manifest right in front of us through the lives of His holy ones.

Our Lord said, "Having eyes do you not see, and having ears do you not hear?" (Mark 8:18). These words apply to many who knew Fr. Solanus, as they apply to many who were in the presence of Jesus. Do they apply to us as well? This is a question we must ask ourselves often.

CHAPTER FIVE

Fr. Innocent Ferstler

Not many laypeople know much about the religious life, but if you are familiar with the distinction between monks and friars, you might know something that is really an open secret: Friars tend to be characters. (Some people have even suggested that I am a character, which is something I've never understood.)

Friars are religious men who live the vowed life, but they work among the people. Franciscans are friars, as are Dominicans. They can easily be contrasted with the Benedictines and Trappists, who are monks and whose lives are usually more removed from the world. Monks are also usually attached to a single monastery for most of their lives, while friars often move from place to place as they are needed.

Both monks and friars enjoy a certain freedom that is common to all people under vows, but the monastic life (the life of monks) keeps them under rather tighter control. Monks, therefore, tend to produce fewer unusual characters than do friars, despite the fact that a monk once wrote a book entitled *Cracks in the Cloister*.

One of the greatest characters I ever met was an old friar who had been a priest in New York City for almost sixty-five years. His name was Fr. Innocent. In the old days many friars had odd names like Fr. Polycarp or Fr. Pancratius, but few friars could ever claim to be as well-named as Fr. Innocent, for in many ways he was among the most innocent people I have ever encountered.

As I said, he was old by the time I met him, and because he had developed hearing difficulties, he had started to speak in a loud voice. And it was a strange voice. Although he was born in the United States, he had a fairly heavy German accent—the accent of a country he had never seen. He came from a family of German immigrants and lived his life first with them and then with German friars. Until the day he died, he sounded vaguely foreign in his native country.

Fr. Innocent was not only innocent, he was in love. He was in love with everybody—the entire human race. To earn Fr. Innocent's love, you didn't have to do anything more than exist. He met people—everyone—with boundless enthusiasm, joy, and appreciation.

And he was a man of prayer. This can be attested to by anyone who lived with him in the last decade or so of his life. Because of his deafness, he often spoke his thoughts out loud, which meant that mental prayer had long before become verbal for Fr. Innocent. As far as he was concerned, he was praying silently. As far as the rest of us were concerned, he was in an audible conversation with God all day long! Every friar knew when Innocent was approaching, even if you couldn't yet see him, because you could always hear him speaking to God (in rather familiar terms) or saying the rosary as he walked.

Every evening we knelt and made our examination of conscience. The entire community was together in the chapel (which was not small). Of course, such an examination is supposed to be silent, and everyone's was—except for Fr. Innocent's. Despite our very sincere intentions not to overhear what he was currently broadcasting, we became aware of his every fault as (notwithstanding many reminders not to) he unknowingly made his daily confession publicly.

It usually went something like this: "Dear Lord, you'd think I'd be doing better than this by now. Sixty years, and I'm trying to do the best I can, but Cajetan [the old priest next to him] is driving me crazy. All he does is eat onions and belch as he walks up and down the cloister." This, as you may suspect, did little to endear him to Fr. Cajetan.

Fr. Innocent offered Mass devoutly and prayerfully but somewhat oddly. Whenever he reached the part in which the celebrant is allowed to quietly mention the intentions of the living and the dead, he would begin a long list, which included such luminaries as President Roosevelt and Mayor LaGuardia—years after they died. Apparently if he had known you or even heard of you, you were assured a perpetual place in his prayers.

Fr. Innocent was a man of conviction when it came to things like politics and religious life, and he would not hesitate to share his thoughts on these matters in the clearest possible way. Perhaps his was not the most sophisticated take on politics, but it was always well-intentioned.

He also had an almost legendary tendency to trip over rules and regulations and occasionally cause embarrassment. His superiors once (and only once) made the mistake of sending him to a special dinner at the home of Cardinal Patrick Hayes, who was New York's archbishop during the early decades of the twentieth century. Trying to brighten up what he took to be dull dinner conversation that night, Fr. Innocent told His Eminence and the assembled clergy that the ladies of the local humane society had recently prevented the police from shooting a dog with a broken leg. When the cardinal agreed that it was probably wrong to keep the dog from being delivered from his suffering, Fr. Innocent laughed loudly and announced, "The policeman couldn't shoot the dog with a broken leg anyway; he has to shoot him with a gun!"

The old cardinal was not amused. He asked Fr. Innocent something along the lines of, "Can you possibly say something a bit more edifying?" Apparently Fr. Innocent couldn't, because for the next fifty years he stayed away from St. Patrick Cathedral. All things considered, this was probably a good move on his part.

Most of us lead rather ordinary lives. We have few great moments, and for the majority of us, that's a lucky fact. Fr. Innocent, however, did have a great moment, one that has been famous for many years among the Capuchins. It was the day that he managed to get himself excommunicated—not once but five hundred times.

We sometimes forget how much stricter religious laws were years ago. Religious orders, especially, had many intricate rules, and it was one of these rules that proved Fr. Innocent's undoing. At that time a woman was absolutely forbidden to enter into any cloistered area of a religious house of friars. If a friar should allow or encourage a woman to enter, he would be immediately excommunicated. (This rather severe legislation would be greatly modified in the aftermath of the Second Vatican Council.)

One rainy day the friars were having a big celebration with hundreds of guests. When dinnertime arrived, the friars adjourned to the refectory to eat their feast piously together, as was the custom. The laypeople, meanwhile, went to eat in the church hall.

Before the friars could even begin their dinner, however, the superior—grim-faced—announced that a disaster had occurred and that Fr. Innocent had brought great disgrace to the community. Astonished, all the friars waited to hear what so great a crime could have been. I think it's safe to say that everyone was astounded to learn that Fr. Innocent had just violated the rules of cloister not once but five hundred times. He was accused of bringing five hundred women into the cloister, incurring a separate excommunication for each and every one of them. To this very day I am convinced that this is a world record.

Innocent was, in fact, guilty. He had made a bold but questionable theological decision and decided that the natural law took precedence in this case. The rain apparently had intensified, and—kindhearted as he was—he didn't want the ladies who were wearing their best clothes and fancy hats to have to go outside and risk getting drenched. Therefore he cheerfully led them through the cloister to the church hall. They arrived dry; he arrived excommunicated.

Early the next morning, the superior sent Fr. Innocent to be absolved by the vicar general, which was technically the only way to rescind the excommunication. Fr. Innocent, in the company of another friar, dutifully made his way to Manhattan and the vicar general's office. By the time he was done relating the tale of the multiple excommunications (which, no doubt, he did in a colorful and very detailed way), the somewhat amazed vicar general was probably at his wits' end. He dismissed the whole matter in seconds, telling Fr. Innocent that there was no need of absolution and to inform his superior that the whole thing was nonsense, that he had never heard such great nonsense before.

Fr. Innocent and the other friar set out for home on the Third Avenue elevated train. They hoped to return quickly;

they did not. As they later told the story, "The angels came down and broke the wheel of the train." Whatever happened, they ended up stranded for two hours at Ninety-Ninth Street. This delay brought Fr. Innocent dramatically back to the monastery at lunch, a meal that seemed to cause trouble for him on a regular basis.

At the sight of Innocent, the superior looked up and instructed the friar reading aloud to stop. "Well," said the superior to Fr. Innocent, "what did the vicar general say?"

Innocent hesitated a moment and then quietly inquired, "Would you mind if I told you privately?"

The superior, however, was adamant. "No," he declared. "You have given this bad example to everyone. Now you must tell what happened publicly."

It was then that Fr. Innocent solemnly announced that the vicar general said that the whole affair was the stupidest thing he had heard in his whole life, dramatically proving that "God shows his judgments against the powerful."

I could really do a whole book of Fr. Innocent stories, but I hope this is enough to give you a taste of this wonderful and unusual traveler along the road to God, a traveler who lived up to his name in every way.

CHAPTER SIX

Rev. Dr. Linn Creighton

I spent a good portion of my youth in Caldwell, New Jersey, a town that was dominated by a huge brownstone Presbyterian church. This is fitting, as the town was named after an early minister of that denomination, the Rev. James Caldwell. Known as the Fighting Parson, he had been a chaplain during the Revolutionary War. When I was growing up, everyone took it for granted that this church was the most important one in town.

When I was fourteen I met a young assistant minister at this church named Linn Creighton. At the time I never suspected he would become a lifelong friend, but he did. Such a thing seemed unlikely, since he was exactly twice my age and, besides, this was long before the days of ecumenism. During that time the clergy of different denominations only got to meet each other when they marched in the Memorial Day parade, usually right behind the band.

At the time, however, I had a great desire to get to know members of other churches. In fact, I like to think I was in the ecumenical movement without knowing it and before it even had a name.

Linn Creighton was different from most of the people I knew. His experiences were unlike those of most people in northern New Jersey, and I found them fascinating. His parents were missionary architects for the Presbyterian Church in China, Turkey, and Lebanon. He attended special American schools in the Near East and in China. Later he attended Harvard University, and then served as a naval intelligence officer during the Second World War, during which his father —still in China—was interned.

After the war Linn began studies at Union Theological Seminary in New York to become a minister. There he met another student, a lovely young lady named Lois Glover, whose goal was to become a minister as well. Lois, however, faced a major obstacle. Although a Presbyterian from her childhood in Scarsdale, New York, she could not be ordained by her church, which at that time included only men in its clergy. As a result Lois was contemplating joining the Congregational Church. This never happened, as the two soon married.

The pair graduated in 1948, and Linn was offered a position as the assistant minister at the Presbyterian church in my town of Caldwell. There he stayed for several years before he was made pastor in the very pleasant town of Flemington, New Jersey, which was not too far away. He guided his flock in Flemington for the next thirty-two years.

In 1956 the Creightons adopted a daughter, Patricia. It is hard for me to believe that she is now not only the mother of two children but a grandmother as well.

Flemington is not very far from Princeton, and so Linn returned to school. He received a doctorate in 1972 from Princeton Theological Seminary. Just three years later, in 1975, Lois's dream of entering the ministry finally came true. The rules had changed in the Presbyterian Church regarding female clergy, and she was ordained.

The custom in the Presbyterian Church is that a minister must be called by God to a specific ministry, and the ministry

Lois received was one to which she was indeed very well-suited. She became pastor to the married students at Princeton Theological Seminary, and eventually was able to preach throughout much of New Jersey.

For many years Linn and I were involved in the most profound and lengthy correspondence of my life. Although he did not, as a rule, enjoy writing long letters, I received from him many single-spaced letters of eight to ten typed pages or more. These were not casual letters but almost always dealt with theological issues, often the differences between Protestant and Catholic theology.

I began receiving these letters when I was a seminarian, and I always wrote back. Our letters were an ongoing debate or discussion. Linn was as firm in his Protestant understanding of things as I was in my Catholic views. Perhaps neither of us ever convinced the other of very much, but I learned a lot from him, and I hope he learned something from me too. These letters led to an increasing closeness, and I was absolutely delighted when both Linn and Lois attended my ordination to the priesthood in 1959.

My ordination day, incidentally, included a somewhat awkward moment that involved Linn. As any Catholic will know, it is customary for people to kneel and ask a new priest for his blessing. This practice, which is so natural to us, does not fit in well at all with the Presbyterian understanding of things, and so Linn—true to his convictions—remained standing while everyone else knelt. I hadn't realized it at the time, as I was giving my undivided attention to each person who had requested a blessing, but apparently Linn's avoidance of kneeling met with some displeasure on the part of at least one old Catholic lady, who voiced her annoyance with this strange man who didn't seem interested in the new priest's blessing.

Linn reminded me of this shortly before his death, when I was visiting him in a retirement home. At that point, so many years later, we could smile about it. Of course, I would never have asked Linn or Lois to kneel under those circumstances, and I would never have thought of asking any of my many Jewish friends to do so either. Obviously, however, not all the Catholics present that day so many years ago felt the same way about this.

Although both Linn and I lived busy lives, always involved in pastoral work and writing, we managed to maintain a friendship that lasted for decades. I consider my friendship with this pair of Presbyterian ministers to be one of the most precious relationships of my life. It opened a door for me into the world of devout Protestants, people committed to a gospel life, whose backgrounds were very different from my own. I can quite honestly say that I never budged in my faith, and I know that Linn never budged an inch in his.

In 1982 Linn retired as pastor. He and Lois moved from New Jersey to Kennet Square, Pennsylvania, to a senior citizen village that was sponsored by the Quakers. Linn has gone home to God now. He died in 2009, and Lois and I have enjoyed the opportunity to remember him and speak of him often since his death.

I was honored to be asked to participate in Linn's funeral service, which took place in the church in Flemington that he had led for so long. It was a very appropriate and proper Presbyterian service, and I was conscious of every aspect of it, determined to do everything right. To my utter astonishment, at the end of the service, the minister offered a spontaneous prayer for Linn on his journey into eternal life. It was practically indistinguishable from a Catholic prayer for the dead—something that years ago would have scandalized Presbyterians and other Protestants, who do not believe in purgatory. I am sure that Linn was staunch in his rejection of this Catholic belief, yet it had slipped into his funeral.

As I was walking away from the church, I thought, "Well, even though neither one of us gave an inch on our theological positions, things have managed to move closer anyway. Thanks be to God, we are closer than we ever were before."

One of my special prayers that I say when I think of entering into the kingdom of God is that I will have my good friend Linn waiting there to greet me. At that point I suspect that our ecumenical endeavors will have reached their conclusion, our theological differences will belong to the past, and only our friendship will remain

CHAPTER SEVEN

Mother Teresa

I remember the evening very well. I had been invited to the home of Catholic author Eileen Egan to meet a nun who had come from India. This all occurred many years ago, back in 1968; it was long before Mother Teresa had become a well-known figure, but I had heard about her vaguely, and I knew that she worked with the poor.

When I got to the right address and walked inside, I discovered myself in a crowded room. I also discovered that my arrival was barely noticed, as all attention was already focused elsewhere. Everyone was clustered around a little woman strangely dressed in—of all things—a white sari. This, it turned out, was the nun I had come to meet.

I learned that each person would have a chance to speak with her individually, and so I got in line to await my turn. The line moved slowly, and it took some time to get to "Mother," which is what everyone called her. When my turn finally arrived, I stood next to this very small woman not knowing what to expect, and then a strange thing happened: Everyone else in the somewhat noisy room seemed to disappear, and I became aware of very little besides the peaceful and gentle face into which I was gazing.

I will never forget her eyes: They seemed to look into my soul. I spoke with her for only a couple of minutes, and I remember asking her to pray for a member of my family who was ill. But by the time I returned to my seat, I knew that in some way I could not quite put my finger on, I had experienced something unusual—perhaps extraordinary. I had spoken to this woman in the midst of a crowded and noisy room, yet my encounter with her seemed intensely private, as if it had occurred in the middle of a huge and open field.

It is my great good fortune and a great grace from God that my meeting with Mother Teresa that night turned out to be only the first of many such meetings. For thirty-five years I received many spiritual messages from this saintly woman, almost always wordlessly, by good example. I was immensely privileged to play a small role in helping her sisters open their house in the South Bronx, their second house in the New York area. I was also able to be of assistance when the sisters founded their first house for the contemplative Missionaries of Charity. I met with Fr. Sebastian, the first priest in the community of male contemplative Missionaries of Charity—priests and brothers—that Mother Teresa founded.

I will always count it a great privilege to have offered Mass for Mother on numerous occasions, but one such celebration of the Eucharist stands out in my mind. It occurred on the last day of her final trip to the United States. After it, she returned home to India, and then only a few weeks later she went home again, this time to God.

As I have said often, along with knowing Fr. Solanus Casey, I count my friendship with Mother Teresa as the greatest single blessing I have ever received. However, even though knowing Mother Teresa was unquestionably a great blessing, I have to admit that it was not always fun, and it certainly was not always easy. Mother could be very incisive, although always in a gentle way. She expected a lot of you, but never any more than she expected of herself.

The problem (if you can really call it that) was that Mother Teresa was able to go forward constantly in the service of others; she never stopped. The rest of us, however, need occasional breaks. We have to catch our breath from time to time.

Like St. Francis, Mother Teresa sometimes didn't realize that others couldn't always follow where she was leading. When someone so deeply spiritual tells you to do something very difficult and matter-of-factly suggests, "Do this for the love of Jesus," you can be stopped dead in your tracks. You know that her experience of love and yours are by no means the same. It's like hearing the captain of a great ocean liner shout over the loudspeaker to you as you desperately paddle your canoe, "It's easy. Just follow along."

I recall that one evening she was—let us say—mildly annoyed with me. Of course she was a perfect lady about it, and the very British manners that she had acquired during her time with the Irish Sisters of Loreto and her many years in India didn't lapse for an instant. She had asked me to do something, and I did manage to get it done, but she had forgotten to give me some special instructions needed to do things in exactly the way she wanted. Not realizing that she had not given me this important information, she gently let me know that I could have done things in a much better way.

We were driving at the time in a car with two Indian sisters, and Mother's rebuke was really very gentle. Somehow, however, getting the needle from Mother Teresa was more painful to me than being harpooned by Captain Ahab on the high seas. By the time we finally arrived at the old house on 156th Street that had become the sisters' convent, I had reached a point of profound discouragement. I said to her, "Mother, I'm sorry to say this, but you're beyond me. I can't handle all this, and I'm going to ask Cardinal Cooke to be kind enough to appoint a different priest as liaison between you and the archdiocese."

I don't know what kind of response I was expecting, but all she did was say, "Come in and sit down." Believe me, when Mother Teresa told you to come in and sit down, you came in and sat down.

I dutifully followed her into the convent, wondering what to expect. Instead of speaking of the events at hand, she asked me, "Why do you think God has chosen you to be a priest?"

Caught somewhat off guard, I hesitated and then mumbled, "I don't know."

Obviously she did not consider this an acceptable response, and she asked the same question over again. Not knowing what else to say, I tried: "Well, maybe it's because He has a sense of humor."

It was then that she gave me what I can only call her special "Mother Teresa look" and said, "You are chosen because of the humility of God. God chooses the weakest and the poorest, the most inappropriate persons to use." Then she said something extremely revealing, which I will never forget: "I pray that my place will be taken by the most unattractive and ungifted of all the sisters. Then everyone will know that this is not our work but God's work. Don't ever forget that you are chosen by the humility of God."

As I closed the door behind me and stepped out into the South Bronx, those words rang in my ears. I can think of nothing more powerful that Mother Teresa could have said to me at that particular moment. It goes without saying that I never asked Cardinal Cooke to replace me as his liaison with her.

After many years of friendship, I went to the Bronx to visit Mother Teresa one last time. I was with Fr. Andrew Apostoli, my confrere. Mother Teresa was planning to return to India later that day, and we didn't want to miss the opportunity to say good-bye. She had become frail by that time, and we knew that she would not be with us much longer. Honestly, we were not surprised to learn of her death only six weeks later.

We offered Mass in the contemplative house for her and her sisters. As always, after the Mass Mother spoke with us. But the conversation that day was different from any I had had with her before. Her words startled me; it was as if I was encountering a person I had never met before. She was laughing and vivacious, and this was not at all typical of Mother Teresa. There had always been a seriousness—even a somberness—about her, which for years I had not understood but often wondered about. Later, long after her death, when I read the book that comprised her letters, I came to understand where that seriousness came from: For thirty-five years she had lived in spiritual darkness—a darkness only a saint could tolerate and transcend.

That evening she told us for the first time how her community had spread. She spoke of the five hundred houses that now existed in over one hundred countries. This was not done as a boast but as a way of sharing wonderful, happy news that she had not spoken of before.

Fr. Andrew and I looked at each other when we came out onto the street. Without saying anything, each of us knew exactly what the other was thinking. It was, in fact, the same thought: Mother was on her way into eternal life. Indeed, this was the case. We had had our final meeting with her in this life; we never saw her again.

My experiences with Mother Teresa over the years certainly convinced me that she is a saint. They also convinced me that she is beyond even that: She is a prophetess. Like St. Teresa of Ávila and St. Catherine of Siena, she is one of those rare people in Church history who permanently change the status quo. After them the Church is different—better than it was before, more nearly what it should be

Mother Teresa's life was completely directed by a single purpose. She lived the gospel at every moment and to its fullest; in this she never wavered. In very vivid terms she showed us what such a life looks like, what a life totally centered on Christ can be, and what He can accomplish in and through us. She showed us that the gospel life does not demand pomp and circumstance or grand ecclesiastical events. Because of her influence Catholics now have a much plainer, more direct approach to such events.

We see this reflected in the life of Pope John Paul II, and in the life of his successor, Pope Benedict XVI. Everyone from the pope on down realizes that it is the preaching and especially the living of the gospel that are at the heart of things. Neither pomp nor elegance, real or imagined, is relevant to this supremely important fact. Mother Teresa, like few saints before her, has drawn our attention back to what is central in Christ's message to us all.

Throughout her life she helped countless people, making God's love real in the lives of untold numbers. This tiny Albanian nun who wrapped herself in a white sari and lived for decades among the poorest people in one of the poorest cities in the world has revealed to us all not only the love but also the humility of God.

CHAPTER EIGHT

Gary

Gary (not his real name) was a thirteen-year-old boy when I first met him. He came—very reluctantly—to Children's Village, a large residential treatment center for boys, which was sponsored primarily by philanthropies but also took a good amount of governmental aid. It was here that I spent many years of my priesthood, and it was here that I met Gary.

He was smart—almost too smart. He was also very angry, and he had no inhibitions when it came to showing his anger. He was the first person I met who was able to swear continuously for five minutes without using the same word more than once—a questionable accomplishment at best.

It was the custom at Children's Village for some of the hard-to-handle boys to be assigned (with my agreement) to work as part of the chapel staff. They did all the chores around the beautiful interfaith chapel, which at that time had only been open a short time. Soon after Gary arrived I knew he would be among this group of chapel boys, and so he was, in almost record time. In those days there were three hundred boys there, ranging from eight or nine years old to sixteen. Children's Village was an institution that did much good against very high odds. Some of the boys were very troubled. Indeed, some were probably beyond help. Gary, however, because of his intelligence, seemed to have a real chance, and as he worked around the chapel, I began to see him change.

The magic of the therapy and care at Children's Village

seemed just the thing for Gary. Step by slow step he started to turn into a productive young man. Naturally, however, deep scars remained, and I knew they would probably remain forever, always making a normal life more difficult for him than it is for most of us. The abused child of a single mother who had been abused herself, he had obstacles to overcome that few people can even begin to imagine.

Gary stayed at Children's Village until he was sixteen years old. At that point he had to leave, and I made arrangements to send him to a Catholic agency for older boys with less severe difficulties, mostly boys out of orphanages. I did my best to keep tabs on him during his time there and was satisfied that he was doing well. Eventually he graduated from high school and was able to go off on his own.

This is a critical time for such boys; for the first time they will not be supervised by adults. It is the moment when you begin to see if the help they have received can really overcome the damage inflicted by their early lives.

One very dark day, after not seeing him for some time, I went to visit Gary. He was then living in a town some distance away. I began the day hopeful, but my hopes were short-lived. It was immediately clear that he was on drugs, and it didn't take me long to learn that Gary had used LSD (a very popular drug at the time) every day for a whole year. This was enormously disappointing and saddening to me. It seemed that all his time at Children's Village and beyond had been wasted. He had become in many ways simply an older version of the boy I had met years before.

Finally I said to Gary very honestly that it would be better for him to go to prison than to continue in the way he was going. At least in prison he would be able to get off drugs. He certainly didn't appreciate my words, but I guess he listened to them: Only two days later he held up four gas stations using an unloaded gun. He was quickly apprehended and brought to trial.

Despite the seriousness of the crime, the judge considered putting Gary on probation because he seemed so promising and intelligent. Although I hated to do it, I asked the judge to give Gary the minimum sentence of three years with time off for good behavior; this would at least get him out of the drug culture that was clearly ruining his life. The judge agreed, and Gary went to jail.

I corresponded with him regularly while he was in prison and sent him books from time to time. Once I sent him a copy of *The Seven Storey Mountain* by Thomas Merton. He read it and was so deeply moved that it led him to a conversion, which he described to me in a beautiful letter. Once again I began to believe that there was hope for this basically good but very troubled young man.

As the date of Gary's release approached, I began to make plans, trying to come up with the situation that would help him the most. A number of years before, I had opened a residence in Brooklyn for young men who were coming out of difficult situations and had no place to go. Called St. Francis House (and now operated under the very excellent direction of Joe Campo), it can accommodate up to fifteen people. Over the years I believe it has done a great deal of good. It was here that I thought Gary should go after being released from prison.

Gary did well at St. Francis House, at least in the beginning. He even started attending St. Francis College, which is also in Brooklyn. I was pleased and thought that perhaps things would finally turn out all right for this young man.

Unfortunately, as is so often the case, as time went on Gary began to lose his way. After a few months I was alarmed to discover that he had left college and gone to work. He also was spending far too much money on flowers and gifts for his girlfriend.

A few weeks passed, and I didn't hear from Gary; then one day the phone rang. The instant I picked it up, I knew it was him, although his voice was hardly recognizable. The words seemed to tumble out of him: "I killed my girlfriend today. I shot her in the street. She was cheating on me."

For a few seconds I didn't know what to say; the shock of his words was so great. Then I managed to tell him, "Stay on the line. Where did this happen?"

He told me that it had happened right in front of a police station, so I immediately contacted the police on another line. I was told that no such event had taken place. Relieved, I returned to Gary and told him that he had imagined the event, that no one had been shot. I tried to calm him down, but he kept insisting that he had killed his girlfriend.

Indeed, what had happened was that he had shot his girl-friend from three feet away, hitting her in the lower part of her leg. She had been able to limp away and had been taken to a Mafia physician for care. The event had never been reported, and the police were not even aware of it.

Gary became more and more excited, telling me that he had committed murder and would now kill himself with the same gun, that he would never go back to jail. I tried to reason with him, but he wouldn't listen. Finally I said to him, "Look, I've taken care of you for ten years. You owe it to me to wait until I can get to you."

Reluctantly he agreed, and I rushed to Brooklyn. I ran up the stairs in St. Francis House to his room. Everything seemed quiet, and I began to feel a vague sense of hope, although I was still very fearful regarding the obvious change in his personality. I knocked on the door and heard his voice asking who was there. I told him it was I and waited for him to open the door. Instead a shot rang out.

The other boys and I rushed him to the hospital, but there was no hope; the bullet had gone straight through his skull. An older person would probably have died almost instantly, but because of Gary's youth and strength, he held on, hovering between life and death, his body struggling desperately to live.

As I stood by the side of his bed in the hospital, I found myself imagining the face of a cloistered nun in front of me, a nun I had seen that very morning when I had given a talk at her convent. The topic had been suffering and sorrow. Only hours before I had made the rather superficial point that no matter what troubles we must face, we should remember that they will finally be overcome. In effect, I had told the nuns that the way to deal with suffering is to cheer up, expecting better things.

My words now seemed foolish—childish—to me as I gazed down at this young man who had suffered so greatly and whose suffering had brought him to the point of death. I thought over and over again of that one elderly sister, who had worn a pained expression as I spoke. I hadn't understood why, and now for some reason I desperately wanted to. Sr. Mary was a good friend of mine but had obviously taken exception to what I was saying. Her face haunted me as I waited with Gary until two o'clock in the morning, the time he died.

As Gary had no family, I had to go to the morgue where they had taken his body and identify it. Afterward I felt badly shaken and deeply saddened. I wasn't sure what to do, but I sensed that Sr. Mary held some kind of key to understanding the events of this painful day. So I called the convent. "Come immediately," she told me. "I understand."

Soon I was sitting across from her, only the convent grille separating us. "I didn't tell you before, but only two years ago one of the closest members of my family took his own life. I was absolutely terrified about his salvation. I worried terribly that he was lost forever," she said.

As soon as she spoke, I found myself blurting out that I was terrified for Gary. If a person should commit suicide knowing what he is doing, it is a terrible sin. The vast majority of people who kill themselves, however, are not capable of such serious sin. The great suffering and pain that it takes to bring one to the point of ending one's life are so extreme that they interfere with the ability to make a free choice or to truly understand the gravity of such an act.

Because of this the discipline of the Church has changed. Years ago a person who committed suicide would have been denied a formal funeral, but since the Second Vatican Council, it is assumed that those who end their own lives are seriously disturbed, making them eligible to receive the last services of the Church. Still I worried for Gary. As Sister and I spoke, I was still filled with fear and a dark sadness.

Then Sr. Mary quoted something by memory from St. Teresa of Ávila. Apparently St. Teresa's brother, Rodrigo, had been in very serious trouble with the law and was at the point of losing his life. In desperation St. Teresa said in a prayer, "Dear Lord, if I were You and it were Your brother, I would see to it that he was saved." Those words lifted a tremendous burden from my shoulders, as they had lifted a similar burden from Sr. Mary's. I have often repeated them to myself, not only regarding Gary but regarding many other people as well.

Sr. Mary assured me that for the rest of her life she would pray for Gary. She went home to God long ago, but I am quite satisfied that her prayers were answered.

CHAPTER NINE

Ruby Davis

I was chaplain at Children's Village for many years, and during that time I learned many things. The first holiday I spent there was Thanksgiving, and I was surprised and saddened to discover that some of the boys who came back to the village after the holiday weekend had not had any holiday dinner. It was because of this experience that I became aware that many poor people living on government assistance are not able to celebrate the holidays in the way that most of us do. It is simply beyond their means to have any sort of holiday dinner at all.

This quickly became an interest of mine, one that has only grown over the past fifty years. I soon started distributing food to the poor at holiday times. With the great help of many friends, I now distribute almost five hundred boxes of food along with five hundred turkeys to an equal number of families just prior to Thanksgiving. We do the same before Christmas and Easter, as well.

It brings us joy to be able to do this. I hope it brings joy to the people who receive the food as well. I know that at least it brings them some real recognition as individuals, something the poor often do not experience. An important part of the distribution is the opportunity to speak with the people to whom we give the food, to get to know them as people, even if only for a few moments.

Our food distributions take place primarily in the South Bronx and began back in the days when that area was at its worst. You may remember that this section of New York was once called Fort Apache and, let me tell you, it was well named. I am pleased to say that this area and similar ones in Harlem have improved greatly over the years, becoming safer and cleaner. Twenty years ago the situation was absolutely desperate; now signs of hope are everywhere.

Out of the big crowd of people to whom we distributed food once came a small, elderly, African-American woman with a huge, sunny smile. Her name was Ruby, and she made it very clear that she didn't want to take any food for herself because she didn't need it. But she did want to take a nice parcel with a turkey for some of her friends who were elderly and poor. We were able to get one of the brothers who were assisting us that day to take Ruby's packages up the street with her to her house. To this day I can still see the tall brother in his habit walking next to the tiny black woman, both laden with food.

After that Ruby became a fixture. Each time we distributed food, she'd show up like clockwork with her big, big smile, always joyful, always buoyant. She never wanted anything for herself but was very concerned about helping others who were too old or sick or feeble to pick up the food themselves.

I became fascinated by Ruby and once asked her what was the secret of her happiness. She responded that her mother had told her years before to stop at noontime each day, think about all the blessings she had, and thank God for them. And Ruby actually did that, every day of her life. She found that this filled her life with joy.

Impressed, I decided to find out more about this unusual woman, so I asked her about her family. At this question her ever-present smile seemed to do the impossible: It got larger.

With obvious satisfaction she launched into a detailed description of her three sons, all of whom were married, doing well, and—she told me proudly—members of different churches in the New York area.

As I pushed a little further, I discovered that Ruby was actually a psychiatric nurse who worked in one of the large hospitals in New York, one I had once worked in as a psychology intern. I also learned she wasn't too pleased with the professional staff at the hospital. It seems they objected to the friendliness of the psychiatric nurses, on the grounds that too much familiarity with the patients could compromise a proper professional distance.

I could understand the objection and that the psychiatric staff would believe such distance to be necessary. But the idea of Ruby being distant from anyone was pretty difficult to imagine. She seemed unable to encounter strangers, as everyone she met immediately became her friend, and she exuded a warmth and friendliness that I have rarely seen matched.

Psychiatric theories aside, I do think that it is not always those who are most professional who are most helpful. I recall that in that same hospital there was an older woman who served meals to the staff in the cafeteria. I watched different professionals, including psychiatrists and psychologists, look for an opportunity to linger at the end of the line so as to have a few moments to speak with the woman who was handing out hash. This uneducated but good-hearted woman had become the psychiatrists' psychiatrist.

Ruby Davis and the woman in the cafeteria teach us something that is very important: Professionalism is a good thing but not the only thing. This is not only true in hospitals, by the way. Members of the clergy usually find out quite quickly that much of the work of God is done not by priests but by other people, usually unassuming people with little or no theological or pastoral training, people who are struggling to find their way to God and are doing their best to love God and their neighbor.

In the eyes of our heavenly Father, we each have our place in life, and we serve as best we can. We must never forget that in the sight of the Lord "many that are first will be last, and the last first" (Matthew 19:30). And we should not be particularly surprised to discover Christ in the warm, sunny smile of a tiny old black woman as she carries her bags of groceries to the poor and forgotten in the South Bronx.

CHAPTER TEN

Bishop James Edward Walsh

I have taught in many places over the years, including Maryknoll Seminary, where I spent several years before most of the dramatic changes that followed the Second Vatican Council were introduced. I remember it as a busy place, and my classes were filled with large groups of seminarians. During those years I was very privileged to meet and come to know Bishop James Edward Walsh, M.M.

Privileged is, in fact, exactly the right word to use when speaking of this man, for he was not just an ordinary bishop. When you met Bishop Walsh, you met someone special: You met a living relic. A missionary in China, he had been imprisoned first by the Japanese during World War II and by the Communists shortly after they took over in the late forties. At some point he had also been taken captive by bandits. But somehow he managed to survive all this without rancor or hostility, which I suspect is not an easy thing to do after languishing in Chinese jails for more than two decades. He was imprisoned for so long that I'm sure most people had abandoned all hope of ever seeing him again.

But God had other plans for Bishop Walsh, and eventually a new day dawned: The Chinese government began to care about what kind of image they were projecting to the international community, and they started to release (and expel) a number of foreign prisoners, many of whom the world had thought long dead. Bishop Walsh was among these; in fact, he was the first. After many years of what seemed like hopeless imprisonment, he was simply brought to the DMZ and allowed to walk into Hong Kong and freedom.

I regularly had the opportunity to chat with Bishop Walsh at Maryknoll, something I always looked forward to. During these conversations, however, I was often aware that I had to be rather careful, as there were certain areas that I knew I must not stray into. Bishop Walsh absolutely refused to denounce anyone—even his captors. He was gentle and charitable, a prayerful man who would never willingly hurt anyone, no matter what the provocation.

Although he would never say anything bad about people, he would certainly express his opinions about ideas. He had a lively mind and an enormous love for the Church. At various points he let me know quite clearly that some of the changes that had occurred as a result of the Second Vatican Council were distressing to him. At times he was also clear in expressing his discomfort with a number of the changes that had occurred at his beloved Maryknoll, changes that, in Bishop Walsh's eyes, made it into something different from what it had always been—less than it once was.

One day, after having known the bishop for some time, I found myself sitting at lunch with him. No one else was at the table, so whatever we said would be very private. This was the moment, I realized, for me to ask him a few questions that I had been wondering about for a very long time. "What was it really like when you were a prisoner?" I inquired, expecting to hear of horrors endured.

Even though it had been some years since his release from prison, Bishop Walsh was still rather gaunt, and I can picture his thin face and white hair as he thought for a moment before answering. "Well, you know, Father, it was like a retreat," he finally said, before smiling gently and returning to his lunch. (It was the custom of Bishop Walsh to address every priest as "Father," although we all would have been delighted to have him call us by our first names.)

After a short time spent trying and failing to discern the similarities between a retreat and a prison term, I tried a little further prodding. I finally got him to say, "Considering the fact that I was a prisoner of war, I was treated rather well. I was in the same cell in the same building for several years, but I was not terribly uncomfortable." He spoke as if he were talking about a hotel that had failed to live up to its reputation.

In near astonishment, I finally asked, "What did they give you for food?"

To which he responded, with a perfectly straight face, "Chinese cooking."

I stared at him dumbfounded, although I can't say I was particularly surprised to learn that the Chinese hadn't flown meatloaf or hamburgers over the border for him.

Bishop Walsh also told me that he spent a great deal of time alone, time which he devoted to almost constant prayer. And although he never was able to offer Mass even once in all his long captivity, he joined his prayers to all the Masses of the world every day without fail. His imprisonment spanned the early and middle sixties, so the Second Vatican Council came and went without Bishop Walsh's even knowing about it. Although he was unaware of the possibility of concelebrating Mass (which was not permitted in the Latin rite prior to the Second Vatican Council), he had spent his time in prison concelebrating all the Masses in the world every day. I am inclined to take that statement very literally and seriously.

One could tell that the new ways of thinking and evaluating things were not those of Bishop Walsh, and some of the events that happened during the late sixties and early seventies troubled him greatly. At times he spoke to me directly about this, and once he even wondered aloud if he might actually have been better off had he remained in prison. No matter what he thought, however, Bishop Walsh remained unfailingly charitable, and his love for the Church never wavered, not even for a second.

What proved to be my last encounter with Bishop Walsh was not an encounter at all; I simply watched him from a short distance away. Yet for years I have seen great meaning in that day. It seems to me to be almost symbolic, a virtual parable. It occurred, of course, at Maryknoll.

A group of very important people—women and men—were walking out the main door of Maryknoll, acting as people act when they consider themselves important. They were talking excitedly about what they were doing, planning new ways to make the Church more effective in the future. From the vantage point of history, we can see that—whatever their intentions—such people ended up accomplishing exactly the opposite of what they wanted to do. Only a small remnant of the Maryknoll that existed during those glorious days, when I used to teach classes of fifty or more seminarians at a time, remains today.

As these important people walked in one direction, Bishop Walsh walked toward them from the opposite direction. He was wearing a black raincoat, which had turned almost green with age, and a baseball cap. His eyes were downcast, and it was not easy to see his Roman collar. If one did not look at him carefully, he could be mistaken for one of the homeless men who often show up at monasteries and seminaries in search of a free meal. As he approached the group of people, not one of them noticed him. No one looked at him or acknowledged him in any way. He was invisible to them.

As I watched, it occurred to me that this unassuming man in the old raincoat was probably the greatest person that any of these others might ever encounter. He was a living saint, a near-martyr, and he was filled with a rare kind of sanctity, virtue, and courage. Bishop Walsh was, to my mind, what a priest should be. Yet the others passed him by as if he were not there at all. They didn't notice him, so intent were they on their bright visions of a future that was never to be. These people were so supremely confident in their personal ideas about the best way to make the Church "relevant" that they weren't even able to see a man who could serve as a model in the rebuilding of the Church—even when he was right in front of them.

Bishop Walsh died not long after that. I consider myself very blessed to have known him, and I continue to wait in hope for the day when someone will stop and look up to notice the extraordinary life and faith of this holy, holy man.

CHAPTER ELEVEN

Sr. Mary Joseph

When I pulled up to the retreat house of the Carmelite Sisters in Soquel, California, I was amazed to see a pert and very stylish woman in her fifties in the process of hefting cases of wine out of a station wagon. She introduced herself as one of the people sponsoring the retreat that I was to lead. The sisters had already told me that it had been organized by some distinguished people, and I knew right away that this woman had to be among them.

She certainly looked and acted the part. With a unique San Franciscan accent, she directed me to tell the retreatants that they "all had to shut up on this retreat. They all live *la dolce vita*, and it will do them some real good to be silent for a change." She then advised, "Don't bother with any of those question-and-answer sessions, because some of them are bound to ask some pretty stupid things, like, 'Is there still a limbo?'"

That was the first of many meetings I had with Ann Miller, one of the most colorful people I have ever encountered. Here was a woman with a real zest for life. Her enthusiasm was so contagious that it was almost impossible to be sad or listless around her; somehow pessimism around Ann seemed almost sinful. This woman was a live wire, and she specialized in doing the unexpected.

After a few years of happy friendship, however, I thought I had seen it all. I believed I knew Ann so well that she could no longer surprise me in any major way. Well, Ann proved me very wrong, for right after that I learned that she was on the threshold of doing the most unexpected thing of her life. She was going to turn her back on her elegant and privileged life and enter the cloister. Ann, then a widow with grown children, was about to become a postulant at a Carmel in Chicago.

The news of this actually broke in the San Francisco newspapers and quickly spread. One of my favorite articles about Ann, written a few years after she entered Carmel, described her as "a dynamic San Francisco socialite with season tickets to the opera, a propensity for silk parasols, and a knack for raising money for charity."[1] It's not an understatement to say that everybody who knew Ann was astonished that such a person could give up so much for the life of the cloister. Many people were very disappointed. They couldn't be blamed for wanting Ann around—nor could they be blamed for finding it difficult to imagine a cloistered nun with a "propensity for silk parasols."

On her sixty-first birthday, a farewell party was held at one of the bigger hotels in San Francisco. It was sponsored by a close friend, and it included no less than six hundred of Ann's other close friends. She danced until two in the morning. At six o'clock Fr. Regis and I celebrated Mass for her. Then we accompanied her to Chicago and to Carmel.

One of the old disciplines of St. Teresa of Ávila makes it very clear that only your mother is supposed to bring you to the monastery. Since Ann's mother was on in years and not at all enthused about the present turn of events, she did not come. Ann was granted a slight bending of the rules, and so Fr. Regis and I became her substitute parents. We walked down the sidewalk with her to the Carmelite convent and said good-bye at the very edge of the property. Ann, who was used to so many possessions, carried only one little bag with her. I can still remember her holding it as she waved at us before entering the Carmel. That was nearly twenty years ago. Ann has never come out.

Others no doubt expected that Ann—who became Sr. Mary Joseph of the Holy Trinity—would become a rather different person under the care and tutelage of the Carmelites and under the inspiration of St. Teresa and St. John of the Cross. Well, they were wrong. On my visits to her over the years, I have found her very much the same—which must be a continuing challenge for the Carmelites, who are (to put it mildly) of a rather different sort. Somehow or other, however, under the grace of God, they all made it work.

Recently Ann celebrated her eightieth birthday. Such events are usually observed in a rather low-key way in cloistered convents, and Ann's celebration was indeed modest, with one notable difference: Every one of her nine children surprised her by showing up at the Carmel for the event. What a beautiful experience that must have been, and how unusual it must have seemed for a cloistered nun to be surrounded by so many offspring.

I'm sure many of her friends in San Francisco originally thought that Ann would be in and out of the convent in record time. But, as I said, this has yet to happen, and since quite a few years have passed, I guess most people have given up hope that she'll leap over the wall and return to California. By this time it must be clear to everybody that—strange as it may seem to some people—Ann really does have a Carmelite vocation. Even the most ardent skeptics, the ones who predicted that she'd be back to San Francisco in weeks or at most in months, have given up hope and realize that she has achieved a kind of quiet that is remarkable—one that was never in evidence in her secular life. She is genuinely happy. I haven't seen in her even the slightest sign of melancholy or sadness.

What does this mean, and what shall we call it? In my opinion the only thing to call it is the action of Divine Providence and grace. But is it really as unique as it seems?

Those who have had the opportunity to read the autobiography of St. Teresa will probably realize that she was also someone you'd not really expect to find in a cloister. St. Thérèse of Lisieux, that other famous Carmelite, certainly does, in her autobiography, give the impression that she was very much made for the cloistered life, but Teresa of Ávila is different. She has a robustness that seems more suited to a different kind of vocation. One of the most famous stories about her involves her falling out of a stagecoach. Getting up from the road, covered in dirt, she said, "Lord, if this is the way you treat your friends, it's no wonder you have so few of them." I don't have too much trouble imagining Ann saying something along those lines.

Rejoice and be glad, because the will of God can be done in all kinds of ways that human psychology and understanding cannot come anywhere close to comprehending. In this we have Ann Miller, Sr. Mary Joseph of the Holy Trinity, as our witness.

CHAPTER TWELVE

Fr. Eugene Hamilton

The death of a young person is seen by all sensitive people as a tragic event. Everyone understands on some level that we must all leave this world sooner or later, but when a young person full of promise and enthusiasm, a person barely on the threshold of life, dies, we feel somehow that it is wrong, unjust, even cruel. Such was the case with Eugene Hamilton.

I felt this sense of the tragic when I first heard of him. He was a young seminarian about to enter his first year of theology after a year of spiritual preparation. It seemed that many good things should await him in this life, but that was not to be the case. He had been diagnosed with cancer, and the cancer was unquestionably terminal.

I didn't really know Eugene Hamilton, but as soon as I could I went to visit him in the hospital. After only a few minutes, I became aware that this was an unusual young man. I was so impressed by him that, after his death, I wrote a book entitled *A Priest Forever* about him, his struggle with illness, and his fervent desire for priesthood. I believed then, and I still believe now, that there are many aspects of this young man's short life that hold lessons for us all.

Despite the sorrow and difficulties of Eugene's death, I have a beautiful memory of him, one that I treasure. I came one night to the hospital to see him. It was after hours, and Gene's parents had already left. He was alone when I looked in. Assuming he was asleep and knowing he needed his rest, I decided not to disturb him. A nurse, however, stopped me as I was about to leave and said, "Father, I think he's awake."

I entered the room and quietly went to the side of his bed. By this point he was the picture of devastating illness, with numerous plastic tubes and blinking monitors in evidence. I spoke his name very softly, half expecting him not to react at all. He answered me, however, very clearly: "Oh, Father Benedict, thank you so much for coming down to see me. I'm so happy that you're here."

We chatted for a few minutes, then I gave him a blessing and left. I was immensely impressed by this young man who was enduring such great trials with a strong faith and quiet courage.

I would see Eugene only once or twice again. I soon had to leave the New York area to give a series of retreats in California, and during that time Eugene died. I was saddened that I had to miss his funeral, but there was no way that I could get home. I learned afterward from the pastor of his church in Haverstraw that his funeral had been exactly what it should have been: a great outpouring of faith and hope. During the funeral there was revealed something that I and only a few others had known: Cardinal John O'Connor had obtained permission from Pope John Paul II to ordain Eugene a priest even though he was just beginning his theological studies.

A date had been set for the ordination, and I planned to be present. But as so often happens, things didn't turn out the way we expected. The doctors had agreed that Eugene had at least six more weeks to live. Thus, we all knew it was important that he be ordained very soon, yet we assumed we had a little time to prepare. God, however, had other ideas.

For some reason I began to feel a persistent urge to call Eugene from California. This feeling became a buzzing in my head; it simply would not stop. As soon as I got the chance, I dialed the number of his parents' home, where he was now living. I was shocked to discover that he had taken a dramatic turn for the worse. It seemed clear that he was rapidly slipping into death.

Eugene's brother Tom, who was with him at the time, didn't realize this. As so often happens in cases such as this one, those who are intimately and deeply emotionally involved cannot see what others can. I told Tom to call the priest. I knew that the time to ordain Eugene had come, so I immediately called Bishop Edwin O'Brien, who is currently the archbishop of Baltimore but was then rector of St. Joseph Seminary, and told him of my fears. He rushed to Eugene's home and ordained the young man a priest on the living room couch.

Eugene's doctor—an Indian gentleman—was present and witnessed the whole thing. Afterward he said to Bishop O'Brien and Eugene's family, "I'm not a Christian; I'm a Hindu. But I want to tell you something: Jesus Christ was here in this room. I saw him lying on the bed."

Later I asked this doctor why he had said this. His reply was, "I don't know why I said it, but I know it is true."

Thus a short life, one that in our eyes ended tragically and too soon, teaches us much. In Eugene Hamilton we have a witness to Christ; we have one who gave Him a pure heart and was willing to accept in faith and love whatever life was to bring. I will never forget the life or the priesthood of Eugene Hamilton.

Along the highway near Eugene's home in Haverstraw, New York, there is a burial plot for priests. From the road one can see an inscription that proclaims an important truth about this seemingly tragic but faith-filled young man. This inscription consists of three simple words: "A priest forever."

CHAPTER THIRTEEN

A Trio of Glimpses

Sr. Mary Dennis

When I was a young priest, one of my tasks for a while was to assist the Sisters of Mercy at their motherhouse in Dobbs Ferry, New York. Basically I would fill in at their chapel when they needed a priest for daily Mass. Then, after celebrating Mass, I would bring Communion to the sisters who were too ill to go to the chapel. A sister holding a lighted candle and a little bell led me through the halls of the motherhouse as I carried the Holy Eucharist. Usually five or six sisters would receive Communion in their rooms.

None of this, of course, was unusual, but the first time I did this I got something of a disturbing surprise. When we arrived at the last room, the sister lying in the bed did not greet me as the others had, nor did she even move. The sister who led me said, "Now, Father, break the precious Host in half. Take that tablespoon and fill it with water. Then float the broken host on the water, and with your other hand open her mouth, and pour the water and the host over her tongue."

I felt quite uncomfortable doing this, but I followed orders and found myself looking into the beautiful Irish face of a woman who appeared to be somewhere in her forties. Her eyes were sparkling and bright blue, but she said not a word and didn't move the entire time. She did, however, make what seemed a kind of half smile when I gave her Communion. This tiny movement—so easy to miss—was both startling and strangely beautiful. Her condition seemed heartrending

I could think of nothing else but this sister as we retraced our steps to the sacristy. When we arrived I blurted out, "What's happened to her?"

The sister who was with me shook her head sadly and said, "That's Sr. Mary Dennis. She's totally paralyzed. When she was only twenty-three, she had a stroke and has been completely immobile ever since, except for one side of her face."

I realized then that the movement I thought I had seen had not been my imagination. The only mobility left to Sr. Mary Dennis was, in fact, the ability to smile or—presumably—to frown with half of her face. I never saw her frown, but every time I brought her the Eucharist, I experienced her smile. Small and subtle, it was a partial smile, and it was produced with vast effort. Yet as time went on, I came to realize that it was a smile filled with great and unaccountable warmth. I like to think that her smile spoke eloquently of hope.

I didn't want to pry, so I asked few questions concerning Sr. Mary Dennis. Over time, however, I did learn more about her. Each bit of new information seemed to deepen the tragedy that she had undergone.

I learned that bandages had to be put on her eyes every night to close them so that she could sleep. I also learned that her back had to be massaged regularly; without such massages she would be unable to move her bowels. Even these basic functions were denied to her. Her condition seemed horribly unfair, and I felt for her deeply, as anyone would. I often marveled at her patience and wondered how she could have endured this for what must have been about half of her life.

Sister's condition made it impossible for her to participate in the life of her community, but the other sisters tried to include her in their prayer life as best they could. Once a year, on the Feast of St. Dennis, Archbishop McGuire would come up to the convent and offer Mass at the door of her room, with as many of the other sisters in attendance as could fit. The sisters had also stretched a large fifteen-decade rosary on the wall opposite the bed, enabling Sr. Mary Dennis to pray the rosary. Although she couldn't hold the beads, she could see and count them.

One day I was walking down a street near the convent and ran into Sr. Mary Dennis's mother, Mrs. Cashin, who wanted to give me a donation to offer Mass for her daughter. The idea that someone who suffered so greatly and so patiently would be in need of prayers seemed inconceivable to me, and I found myself saying, "Why in the world does your daughter need a Mass offered for her? She'll go straight to heaven, like the angels."

Sister died not long after I first saw her, and this surely was a blessing. Almost exactly one half of her life was spent in this terribly difficult, almost horrifying state. She was a soul virtually entombed in a body, and I truly believe that her death was a release into great freedom and joy, a joy that she had anticipated patiently and faithfully throughout her years of silent immobility, a joy that I had been blessed to see foreshadowed in her smile.

The Elephant Man

About twenty years or so ago, a Broadway play became quite popular. It was later made into a film, which also did very well. Called *The Elephant Man*, it told the true story of Joseph Merrick, a man in Victorian England who was so severely disfigured that his appearance barely seemed human. Shunned and rejected by many, Joseph Merrick was ridiculed as the Elephant Man and even displayed as such in sideshows. He suffered greatly for much of his life. In the play, however, people were given the opportunity to look beneath the surface, to see past the unattractiveness of this gentle man's physical appearance to his humanity.

I often celebrated Mass at a cloistered convent. Besides the sisters, who sat behind their grille, a fair number of laypeople would attend. One day I had reached the point at which I was to give Holy Communion to the congregation. As the people started to approach the altar, I received a shock.

Suddenly in front of me, preparing to receive, was an elephant man. It was as if Joseph Merrick had stepped out of the play or out of history and now stood before me, waiting to receive the Body and Blood of Christ. I was so startled that I think I gasped, and when I held out the Host to him, I fumbled for a few seconds, trying to determine precisely how I could manage to put it into his misshapen mouth. After Mass I looked for him, but he had disappeared.

A couple of days later, however, I was back at the convent, and he showed up again. This time I was prepared, and when I gave him Holy Communion, I whispered for him to wait for me after Mass, although I admit that I wasn't sure he'd do so. As it happens, he did wait, and we began to speak.

It immediately struck me that sitting before me was a very gentle, quite ordinary man. Despite the terrible catastrophe that had befallen him, he did not seem to show great grief or profound struggle. He did explain to me that he had been dismissed from school after the fourth grade because his appearance had been disturbing to the other children, and they had made fun of him. I also learned that he had spent his whole life "working in the packaging industry." This meant that some company sent to his home many things that had to be packaged. He did the work at home, and when it was completed, the company picked it up. In this solitary, isolated way he supported himself.

Clearly he was cut off in many ways from other people, yet somehow or other this man did not present himself as a person who had undergone great tragedy. In a humble, matter-of-fact way, he accepted his unusual situation with a great deal of equanimity. He seemed at peace with it in a way that few people would be.

After that first conversation I made it a point to speak to him whenever possible. After a while I managed to get used to his face, but I must admit that this took some time and effort. We talked about many things that he was interested in, many things he wished he could do. Most of them were beyond his grasp, of course, because his life was one of isolation from others. At least he was able to live with his single brother, and in that way he was not completely cut off from companionship.

I was eventually transferred and no longer had the opportunity to see him. I will always remember, however, this man who accepted a life that seemed so unacceptable, who bore a terrible cross with grace, peace, and faith. I often think of this ordinary man who was really very extraordinary, and for the rest of my life I will remember one question that he put to me: "Father, do you think that, after I die and go to heaven, I'll still be like this, or will I have a real face?"

It was difficult for me even to speak to answer this question. When I finally found the words, I reassured him that his face and body would, indeed, be perfectly healed. I hope he believed me, and I hope that he understood that through every moment of his life, our heavenly Father saw him in his true beauty and loved him deeply because of his great faith and trust.

The Altar Boy

Part of the reason for writing this book is to show that people who have serious problems or misunderstandings are no different from the rest of us and certainly no less loved by God. After half a century in the priesthood and nearly as many years as a psychologist, I have become very aware that there are some people whose problems simply cannot be helped in any direct way by the institutional Church—except, of course, by the support of the Church's constant prayer. The will to help is certainly there, but the institutional Church is not God, and she sometimes lacks the knowledge or understanding to confront a specific problem immediately.

Occasionally there are people whose circumstances are so unusual that no structures yet exist to deal with them. Sometimes they have been drawn into difficult situations that are simply not acceptable to the teachings of the Church, even though these people strive mightily to be devout Christians. Sometimes such people, through their own choices, complicate what is already an ambiguous situation.

I have often heard Catholics say of another that he is "wrong in the eyes of God." This may very well be true, but we must always guard against arrogance in saying this. The fact of the matter is that we cannot always be sure. Who among us really knows what is in the infinite depths which the eyes of God can see? We can see through the eyes of the Church, and we should always be very seriously guided by this, but we must never forget that we do not see with the eyes of God. We must never try to limit God to what we can see or understand.

One expects certain questions in certain situations. Different groups will have very different concerns. When I speak I often can tell by looking at the people sitting in front of me what kind of questions they will ask. I have spoken often to cloistered nuns over the years, and I can assure you that one of the topics they do not regularly dwell on is that of transgendered people. Yet one day, in just such a setting, one of the sisters asked me a very pointed question on this topic. I was slightly taken aback but assumed that someone in her family was facing this problem.

Although there is as yet no papal teaching about this, the general belief put forward by moral theologians is that it would be wrong to attempt to change one's sex and particularly to use surgery to accomplish this. There is a principle of preserving unity of the personality and body. We must also recall that sex-change surgery is misnamed: A person's sex is not changed as a result of it. One might be made to resemble the opposite sex and to take on certain characteristics of that sex, but one still has the chromosomal nature one was born with: XX for women and XY for men. This is what determines our sex, and nothing in medical science can yet alter it.

All this may seem absolutely obvious, and it is obvious from the point of view of most of us, because most of us never feel estranged from our sexual natures. We are content with the bodies we have. Yet there are people who feel trapped in bodies that seem to deny the persons they feel themselves to be. There are few such people, but they exist, and their suffering is sometimes great.

From a practical point of view, very few clergy have had an opportunity to speak extensively to people who feel they belong to the wrong sex. This is very different from same-sex attraction, which is also something that a person has rarely chosen but has frequently had from very early in life.

At the time that I was asked this difficult question in the cloister, I had never even spoken to a person who had attempted to change gender. Such things were far outside my experience. But the sisters had asked me this question at the grille, and they wanted to hear an answer.

I certainly did not want to be glib, but in retrospect I'm afraid my answer must have come across that way. I said, "Psychological problems can't be settled by knives. Surgery is not the answer." Although no one said anything more about this, I left that day with the inescapable feeling that I had said something that troubled people deeply, that may even have been hurtful.

Sometime later I received a letter from a young man who claimed to have heard from the sisters of my comments that day. He protested my remarks in a way that was passionate yet calm and very respectful. He said that I had failed to understand the problems of transgendered people. He also asked to speak to me, and I agreed.

The next time I came to the cloister, the young man was there, and I was introduced to him. He wore a neatly trimmed beard and was dressed very appropriately. To me he looked to be about twenty-four years old, and he seemed the picture of a devout young Catholic man. He served as altar boy at Mass, performing his duties well and with obvious devotion.

When the Mass ended we sat down to talk privately. I wasn't sure what he was going to say to me, but I am absolutely sure that I wasn't expecting to learn that he had been a member of a teaching order of religious sisters. To tell you the truth, I was never more surprised in my entire life. This person turned out, in fact, to be older than I had thought. As a young woman she had felt called to the religious life and had spent a short time as a postulant. But she had been deeply troubled, feeling in a very basic and profound way that she was not a woman at all but a man.

After leaving the convent she eventually underwent sex-change procedures, which included surgery and extensive hormonal therapy. She now lived as a man, feeling peace for the first time, and also feeling that she had finally become the person she was meant to be from the beginning. This young woman assured me that she was leading a devout and chaste life. I have no reason to doubt this.

As we make our way through life, we must never be hasty in judging unusual situations. Humanity is extraordinarily complex. I am sure there will be a number of people reading this book who, because of a variety of psychological experiences or other reasons, don't fit neatly into any of the usual categories. There is one category, however, into which we all fit: We are all made in the image of God, and we are all beloved of God. We must remember this as we confront marriages that are invalid and homosexual relationships, which are unacceptable to Catholic teaching and to Scripture. We must remember that we often don't see the whole picture, for we cannot see with the eyes of God. The Church sees very deeply but cannot see everything.

Our Lord went out of His way to show concern and kindness to people who did not observe the moral law. He saw beyond what others saw and accepted those whom others despised. Many rejected Mary Magdalene as a great sinner, but He saw that she could also be a great saint. He often showed great love for the publicans and harlots, even declaring that they would enter the kingdom of God before the punctilious observers of the Law (see Matthew 21:31).

This is an important lesson that we must never forget. I am greatly blessed in having received the gift of faith; I have thus found peace in my life by seeing with the eyes of the Church. We must always be aware that the Church speaks for Christ in matters of faith and morals, but we must also remember that the eyes of God are unique, and they see more deeply than we can imagine. The eyes of God see all things, and God understands what none of us can even begin to comprehend.

The three people I have described in this chapter challenge, in one way or another, our easy understanding of the divine will. What happened to Sr. Mary Dennis ought never to have happened to anyone, as far as we can understand. The same is true of the Elephant Man. Both lived lives of extreme, seemingly cruel isolation, yet both of these people accepted with great faith and trust the misfortunes that befell them.

The third person also felt imprisoned within her body, and she embarked on a path that few can understand and fewer can agree with. But I can assure you that the person I met loved God and was sincerely trying to lead a chaste Christian life, even though that life was very different from what we have come to expect.

How exactly does God view these people and their difficult physical and psychological trials? None of us can ever truly know. But one thing we can know with perfect certainty is that He always looks at them with love.

CHAPTER FOURTEEN

Cardinal Terence Cooke

Although I have long been involved in the cause of beatification of Cardinal Terence Cooke and was even its diocesan postulator, I do not want to write here about my friend Cardinal Cooke as a possible saint of the Church. Instead, in this little recollection I prefer to concentrate on a few incidents that touched me deeply. Here I hope to introduce you to Terry Cooke, the man.

Nearly twenty years ago I wrote (with Lutheran pastor Terrence Webber) *Thy Will Be Done*, a biography of the cardinal. In that book we attempted to draw a spiritual portrait of a very good and holy man. I wanted people to understand the depth of the cardinal's spirituality and the breadth of his kindness to others. I was always very aware that I was not writing the life story of a "great personage." He was in many ways an ordinary man placed in an extraordinarily difficult situation—one he handled very well.

Terence Cooke was a monsignor when I met him. This was at the beginning of the ecumenical period, and I had to go to him to obtain permission to preach in Protestant churches and in synagogues. He kindly arranged such permissions for me. When it came to one speaking engagement that was rather sensitive, he very characteristically warned me "not to swing at every pitch." Cardinal Cooke loved baseball and often used analogies from this sport and others when making a point. I remember and make use of this wise advice even today.

As a young priest Terence Cooke had been assigned to Catholic Charities. He was especially involved with the care of teenagers and youngsters; his first assignment was to serve as chaplain of a large orphanage. This was exactly the kind of work he most enjoyed and at which he excelled. He loved and understood young people, and they loved him.

From those early days, all the way through his time as archbishop of New York, he was always a gentle, humble, unassuming kind of man, constantly concerned about others, often to the point of forgetting his own needs. In all the years I knew him, he never considered himself anything but an ordinary person. At times this made people underestimate or even dismiss him. I saw people (the type who considered themselves intellectuals) demean him behind his back or even give him a cool reception to his face. Many others can tell you of such things. Terence Cooke never complained about this; he was far too kindly and gentle for that.

He was a prince of the Church and in charge of one of the most important archdioceses in the world, yet these facts almost seemed to surprise him. In a way Terence Cooke was too humble to see the wisdom in his own selection as cardinal. One could see that the weight of his office sometimes hung heavily on him, yet he went about his duties with a cheerfulness and optimism that was born of a simple yet very profound faith. When he returned to New York from Rome, he was expected to have a celebration, and so he did, but it was a uniquely Terry Cooke kind of celebration. He sat on the steps of St. Patrick Cathedral for hours, meeting and speaking with anyone who wanted to talk to him. To him this was the most natural way to celebrate becoming a prince of the Church.

After Cardinal Francis Spellman's death, there was a great deal of speculation as to who the next archbishop would be. All the important names in the American Church were mentioned, but few people thought of Cardinal Spellman's vicar general, Terence Cooke, who was then only forty-seven. His good friend Bishop Patrick Ahearn tells of the night before the new archbishop's name was to be announced.

He and Terence had gone out to dinner with a group of other priests and had come back late to the cathedral, where both were living. Instead of going inside, Terence Cooke suggested a walk around the block. Just after midnight he looked at his watch, stopped, and then asked his friend who he thought the next archbishop might be. Bishop Ahearn mentioned a few names, but Terence Cooke shook his head and said, "Pat, it's me." Then, overcome with emotion, he began to weep. "They're going to put me on the cross and never take me down," he said.

I think the timing in this story shows something important about Cooke. He had been instructed not to give word of his selection until the next day. He was the sort of person who took such obligations seriously. So he waited until midnight, the moment the new day began, to unburden himself to his best friend.

The next morning the news was announced to the world. Bishop Ahearn got up early and knocked on the new archbishop's door, expecting to find his friend upset and frightened. Instead a smiling and confident Terence Cooke opened the door.

"Don't worry, Pat. Even this will be all right. God will get us through," the new archbishop said. He was repeating words he had heard as a boy, words his father had spoken to him shortly after his mother died.

Cardinal Cooke probably never wanted to be an archbishop —or even a bishop for that matter—but he saw his position as a task he had been given by God. He was archbishop during a particularly difficult time and faced many trying moments, yet he always remained calm. He trusted completely in God and relied entirely on prayer.

The prayers of Cardinal Cooke were more often than not the simple devotional prayers common to the Irish Catholic people. He showed how powerful such devotions can be during a time when many people disparaged them. He later collected many of these prayers and others in a book entitled *Prayers for Today*. Known as "The Little Red Prayerbook," it continues to play a role in the spiritual development of many, more than a quarter century after the cardinal's death.

Prayer might have come naturally to Terence Cooke, but conflict certainly did not. He was so kindhearted by nature that he would go to almost any lengths to avoid hurting people. As archbishop, however, there were times when conflict could not be avoided. He had to take positions that would be unpopular with one group of people or another. I knew him well, and I have no doubt that each time he had to offend or disappoint someone, he felt real pain. But just as he had accepted becoming archbishop, he accepted this pain as his lot, never speaking about it or showing others how much certain things hurt him.

And he never failed to do all he could to minimize any pain he might cause others, even if that would sometimes increase the pain he himself was to undergo. I remember many instances of his going out of his way to make sure that people who seemed to be left out or contradicted by certain decisions didn't feel rejected by either him or the Church. Despite this he would never compromise Catholic teaching, and he never wavered in his support of the Church. I think it is accurate to say that in whatever he did, he worked for the good of the Church.

I was blessed to know Cardinal Cooke over many years, so I have many memories of him, the most precious of which comes from a very difficult time. A few days before his death, he invited me to visit him for what we both knew would be the last time. By then he was confined to his bedroom in the cardinal's residence, and he was dying of leukemia, brought on by years of chemotherapy treatments for cancer. He had chosen not to go to a hospital but stayed in his own room with round-the-clock care. He had the Blessed Sacrament exposed before him and was in virtually constant prayer. Already his hands were dark purple, showing the dramatic progress of the disease; it was as if his hands had already started to die.

When I walked in I wasn't sure what to expect, but I found him amazingly warm and enthusiastic about things. He was looking forward to going home to God, with great peace and unshakable trust.

I did what people do under such circumstances: I attempted to say something consoling. Somehow or other, though, things reversed themselves, and before long I realized that it was he who was consoling me.

After a very precious half hour, I said good-bye to him, knowing that I would never see this dear friend again in this world. We actually spoke about meeting again on the other side. As I came down the steps of his residence, I could not see where I was going; tears were streaming from my eyes, and I couldn't stop them.

I learned that President Ronald Reagan and his wife had just been in to see the cardinal. Coming down the same flight of stairs, the president had said, "What a man. I've never known a man like this." All the cardinal had wanted to speak of was the needs of others, especially the poor and children. He seemed to give no real thought to his own situation, to his illness and rapidly approaching death.

Knowing Terence Cooke as I did, I can understand that. He would unquestionably have seen his own death as he saw so many things, as an act of Divine Providence. He would have had no time for regret; indeed, he would have seen no reason for regret. He was living out in a very beautiful and spiritual way his own episcopal motto: *Fiat voluntas tua* (Thy will be done). This was not just a saying for him. It was a way of life. Even as he approached death he continued to do what he had always done: accept the sometimes harsh realities of life as God's will. In so doing, he was able to find in these difficult moments a mysterious part of God's love. The words "Thy will be done" are written loudly and consistently over the events of his life and death. For this and for many other reasons, I consider it among the great blessings of my life to have known this man who seemed so ordinary yet lived so extraordinarily holy a life.

CHAPTER FIFTEEN

Mother Mary Aloysius McBride

Visitors who are unfamiliar with New York City are invariably impressed and sometimes even overwhelmed by the huge buildings, as well as the many and varied institutions that are crowded into the small area we call Manhattan. Manhattan, of course, is an island, one that is actually a single huge piece of rock. It is this rock that supports New York's skyscrapers; the foundations that are blasted into the rock of Manhattan are so solid that buildings with huge numbers of stories can be constructed on top of them.

Among the many institutions and enterprises in Manhattan is one that may not look as spectacular as many of New York's large buildings; it is one that I consider very special nonetheless. On York Avenue and Seventy-Second Street sits a handsome, red brick, twenty-story building, the Mary Manning Walsh Home.

This nursing home gives wonderful and compassionate care to the elderly. It is an institution that treats its residents with dignity and love. In short, it is the kind of place where we would all be blessed to spend our final years on earth.

Administered by the Carmelite Sisters for the Aged and Infirm, the Mary Manning Walsh Home has been a model for the care of the elderly for many years, and it is known worldwide. There are many reasons for this. Here we will discuss but one: Mother Mary Aloysius McBride, O. CARM.

Tiny in her brown Carmelite habit, Mother Aloysius had

the bright blue eyes of her Irish ancestry and a shy, almost girlish smile that was a delight—in part because one didn't see it too often. She was a sister of the old school, very proper, very formal, very reserved, very much an unstoppable force of nature. Mother Aloysius, by the way, built the Mary Manning Walsh Home as surely as if she had laid every brick herself.

Born in County Tyrone in Ireland, Helen McBride came to the South Bronx as a small child, and although far from the land of her birth, she would never completely lose the soft accent of her native country. Part of a large and deeply religious family in the South Bronx, she knew intense sadness at an early age. Her mother died when Helen was in her early teens.

In order to help keep the family together, Helen had to go to work. But within a few years, the unexpected happened: She was able to realize her dream of entering the Carmelite Sisters for the Aged and Infirm with her younger sister, who became Sr. Stephen.

This community was new and its future uncertain. Founded by the Servant of God Mother Angeline Teresa McCrory, O. CARM., in 1931, the Carmelite Sisters for the Aged and Infirm had few members when Helen became a postulant. No one could predict that it would one day care for hundreds of thousands of people in nursing homes throughout the United States. Along with the Little Sisters of the Poor, this congregation is probably the largest institution for the care of the elderly in the New York area.

Among the earlier sisters to join Mother Angeline's community, Helen became Sr. Mary Aloysius, later confessing that she didn't even know how to spell the name that she had been given. In joining the Carmelites, she began a life that would benefit many and transform the way we care for the elderly.

Sr. Aloysius' talents were soon recognized, and before long she was called "Mother" and put in charge of one Carmelite institution after another, culminating in the construction of the Mary Manning Walsh Home. Her imprint can be found everywhere there, from the warm and inviting atmosphere to the many programs that keep the residents involved–things ranging from musical concerts to an annual "night at the races." Her goal was to care for the elderly but never to look down on them, to see them as real people and often reposito-ries of wisdom and experience.

Like so many sisters, Mother Aloysius possessed a quiet fearlessness and a serene determination. Once in the early seventies, the Mary Manning Walsh Home, along with all the other nursing homes in the city, was going through a strike of workers responsible for cleaning, maintenance, and laundry. The sudden loss of staff in these areas crippled many an insti-tution in the city, but not Mary Manning Walsh.

Mother Aloysius by this time had developed such a large and loyal following, consisting of the family members of pres-ent and former residents, that she simply went to the phone and called them. In hours doctors were mopping floors, lawyers were bringing trays of food to residents, and women in diamonds and designer clothes were hulling strawberries and making soup in the kitchen.

When a picket line in front of the nursing home threatened to become rowdy, Mother walked outside wearing her full, floor-length Carmelite habit. She said nothing; she looked at no one. She simply stood there peacefully, her arms folded beneath her brown scapular. One by one the picketers quieted. When order had been restored, she turned around and went back into the building and back to work.

Mother Aloysius knew everyone. How a sister came to be on a first-name basis with ex-mayors of the city of New York, political commentators, businessmen, and people in the world of the arts is indeed a mystery, but somehow she knew them all. I was often astonished at the people she met and knew. In a quiet way she was one of those people who hold the city of New York together, who make it a truly human place.

Mother Aloysius' main claim to fame will always be her care of the elderly; she even testified before Congress regarding elder care laws. But she had another accomplishment as well, one that grew directly out of her long-standing friendship with Cardinal Terence Cooke.

To say that Mother Aloysius was perceptive is a great understatement: She had the ability to read people in a way that could sometimes be dismaying. From the beginning she sensed something special about the young priest who would one day be New York's archbishop. She saw in his quiet kindness and unfailing gentleness something that others didn't see, something out of the ordinary. She never lost this belief, and after Cardinal Cooke's death in 1983, hers was among the first voices raised for his canonization. When Cardinal John O'Connor formally opened the cause of his canonization, Mother Aloysius became foundress and first coordinator of the Cardinal Cooke Guild. As such she was essentially in charge of the cause for many years.

Starting her work with a few documents and lists of names kept in a shoebox, Mother Aloysius began to establish a network of supporters. Soon the Cardinal Cooke Guild had members throughout the world. She also brought to the task a small army of devoted volunteers, many originally from the Mary Manning Walsh Home, and these volunteers—out of devotion to Mother as much as to Cardinal Cooke—have worked steadily for over twenty years. Her work, now ably carried on by Patricia Handal, has made this cause one of the leading efforts in the United States for a cause of canonization. This is especially noteworthy since Cardinal Cooke has been dead less than thirty years.

Mother Aloysius was born in Ireland, but she became a true New Yorker. The wealthy, the important, bishops, and tough businessmen all admired her ability, perceptiveness, and aplomb in the midst of this great and confusing city. Those of us who knew her well also admired her unshakably strong faith, her dedication to others, and the great sacrifices she made for those in her care. She organized a cause of canonization, but it is not far-fetched to say that there may be such a cause for her one day.

In the history of the Church there are many great nuns. Most of them did their work in rural areas and quiet cloisters, in hospitals and schools or orphanages. Yet in the midst of the hustle and bustle of New York City stood a prim and proper Carmelite in the habit of St. Teresa, regularly and quietly accomplishing things that no one else could. She was the quintessential New Yorker, she was a woman of great love and compassion, and she was every bit as strong as the rock of Manhattan.

CHAPTER SIXTEEN

Frank Sheed and Maisie Ward

I regret that many intelligent young Catholics are not familiar with Frank Sheed and his wife, Maisie Ward. These are names that only a few decades ago every literate Catholic could be counted on to know. Their company, Sheed and Ward, published hundreds of high-quality Catholic books, and the two of them were prolific writers themselves (a combination that is rarer than you might think). They were also great apologists for the Church. Indeed, for a time they seemed to be the best-known Catholic couple in the English-speaking world.

Originally from Australia, Frank moved to England as a young man. There he met and married Maisie. Although his original intent was to study law, both Frank and Maisie came to believe that the needs of the Church should take priority. They turned to the Catholic Evidence Guild, and the former law student and his rather upper-class English wife were transformed into street preachers, standing on corners proclaiming the truths of the Catholic Church to all who would listen.

This was only the beginning; before long the speaking was supplemented by writing, and their publishing company was born. After a good number of years as successful publishers in Britain, Sheed and Ward—both the company and the couple—moved to the United States. I don't hesitate to say that this was definitely England's loss and our gain.

The Sheeds are a remarkable couple, and they were remarkable individually as well. Yet if you met them, you would not always realize that. Despite their outstanding literary and personal qualities, they were absolutely indifferent to any kind of material success. Their physical needs were few, and in their old age they lived in a very modest apartment in Jersey City (a town that I am very fond of).

One day I got a call from Frank. He and Maisie were wondering if I "might possibly do them a great favor." According to him, they needed a little help and were hoping I might be able to send one or two staff members from our retreat house to give them a hand. Of course I agreed without a second thought, and then I asked Frank what the problem was.

As casually as if he were describing a leaky faucet, he told me, "Oh, nothing much really. It's just that our ceiling seems to have come crashing down onto our floor." What Frank was too charitable to mention was that a drunken neighbor upstairs had fallen asleep in his bathtub and neglected to turn off the water.

Off we went to Jersey City, where the apartment looked like a disaster area. We spent the rest of the day digging them out, carting large quantities of fallen plaster from Frank and Maisie's home and uncovering what was left of their furniture.

This is obviously the sort of thing that would bother anybody and greatly disturb most people. Frank, however, found the whole incident amusing. He seemed almost to enjoy standing in the midst of domestic destruction. Despite falling ceilings and drunken neighbors, both he and Maisie resisted friends who tried to get them to move to a better location. The Sheeds had a specific aim, which they never abandoned: It was to live the gospel, and so they thought it only natural to live with the poor—despite the inconveniences that such a way of living might bring.

I am very fortunate in that I knew the Sheeds for years. I first met them when I was the youngest member of the Catholic Evidence Guild, the same group they worked with in London. This fine organization existed in many large cities, and the Sheeds never ceased to support it. Founded by the great Fr. Vincent Nabb, O.P., it was always a fascinating group, but the most interesting people among them were Frank and Maisie.

It would be difficult to decide which of the two was more charming or the greater intellectual. Yet there never seemed to be the slightest hint of competition between them. Frank was always delightful, entertaining, and maybe even brilliant; Maisie, too, was always impressive—and very English, with no holds barred. I once heard someone ask her about a particular Catholic book making the rounds at that time, a book well thought of by many. In her very British way, she simply dismissed it as "ghaaaastly." The word seemed to go on forever, as did her obvious displeasure.

Books published by Sheed and Ward, however, were never ghastly but were almost always excellent. Announcements of their books and occasional reviews were published in a periodical called *Our Own Trumpet*, which many readers (myself included) very much enjoyed.

With typical English reserve, neither Frank nor Maisie revealed very much about their family or their private life, but they were very proud of their son and daughter, Wilfrid and Rosemary. Their son carried the name of esteemed apologist Wilfrid Ward, who happened to be his grandfather. After Frank's death his son published a study of his parents called *Frank and Maisie, a Memoir with Parents*. Unfortunately it was disappointing to me and to others who had known them.

During the turbulent times of the 1980s, among many new ideas that were in the air was one that suggested some Catholic laymen be made cardinals. (The proper word used in regard to the appointment of a cardinal is that he is "created.") Theologically there was no problem, as this dignity has no connection with ordination. Someone suggested that Frank be made a cardinal, and many supported this idea.

Frank was aghast. He shot back immediately: "There's never going to be a Frank Cardinal Sheed unless there's a Maisie Cardinal Ward." It was very clear that Sheed and Ward was a full partnership.

As it turned out, lay cardinals were never created, so the problem never arose. The question that long concerned me about Frank Sheed, however, was not whether he'd become a cardinal but whether he'd become a saint. All things considered, this seemed a more likely prospect.

During a time when there was a severe attack in the media against religion in general and the Catholic Church in particular, I recall the very positive, calm witness of Sheed and Ward, which was intelligent, faithful, and persuasive. Based on this and many other reasons, we once asked Frank to offer a retreat at Trinity for priests. With some hesitation he agreed. His opening remark to the clergy was typical: "It seems to me that my giving a retreat to priests is a violation of the natural law."

In his old age, especially after Maisie's death (I gave her the last sacraments), Frank became increasingly meditative and even contemplative. He was staying for several days at our retreat house when I found him sitting, just staring out at Long Island Sound. Foolishly I asked, "Frank, would you like me to find something for you to read?" In a very philosophical way, he smiled and said, "Benedict, I've already read it all."

The Catholic Evidence Guild is still going strong in New York. The world has changed quite a bit, and the struggles and debates between religious denominations concerning religious belief have quieted a great deal. The big problem right now is a lack of interest or at least a lack of commitment to religious truth. In today's world it is more difficult than it once was for apologetics, particularly the type used by Sheed and Ward, to be heard and considered. This is a great loss.

I hope and pray that the day of great apologetics will come back and that there will be a beautiful renewal through the books that were written and published by this remarkable couple, who were extraordinary human beings and splendid Catholics.

CHAPTER SEVENTEEN

Karen Killilea

Every morning for thirty-five years, Karen Killilea has entered my office. I never hear a sound, for she moves silently to her desk. There she sits in her wheelchair, surrounded by pictures of cats and saints, of prelates and puppies, and she begins her day's work answering my phones and responding to the bewildering assortment of requests that flood relentlessly into my office. If you've ever called me, it's a safe bet to say that you've spoken with her. You may not know her name, but you know her voice. It's the voice with a smile.

Is Karen the greatest receptionist in the world? Perhaps not, but she's among the top five or ten.

Years before I met Karen, I had heard of her. Like many people back then, I almost thought I knew her, but I was wrong. My original knowledge of her, you see, came from a book written by her mother and simply entitled *Karen*. This was the beautiful story of a baby born three months premature, of a young girl with cerebral palsy. It is really a story of the triumph of faith and love, of obstacles overcome. I found it very moving, and so did many others. It sold over a million copies.

The book made Karen famous—but unhappily so. During my first encounter with her, I was eager to discuss the book and surprised to discover that Karen did not want to speak of it at all. I came to realize that she—quite reasonably—wants to be known as herself, the person she's become, rather than the picture that appears in this biography. The book touched so many people that some of them would actually show up at the Killilea house unannounced, expecting to meet and talk to Karen and her family. Sometimes even priests were guilty of this. Amazingly, such people seemed unaware that they were intruding into the private life of a family.

I got to know Karen fairly well, but I never dreamed she'd ever work for me. Odd things happen, however, and sometime later Karen was looking for a job at the same time that I was looking to hire someone. The telephone was becoming overwhelming and was distracting me from my work. I needed a receptionist, someone to field my calls, to give me a little privacy, to stand between me and the rest of the world—at least for a few days each week. So Karen came to my office, and a working relationship began that has lasted for three and a half decades.

Over the years I've watched her in action, deftly handling many difficult people and situations on the telephone. People who are seriously disturbed sometimes call; others demand impossible responses, and they're the ones who usually won't take no for an answer. She treats people with kindness and good sense, and she has patiently listened to innumerable tales of woe.

Karen also deals with many important people, including members of the hierarchy. From time to time I've heard her calling someone by a nickname on the phone. After all these years I've ceased to be surprised when I discover that those nicknames sometimes belong to archbishops or cardinals. She's been handling so many different types of people for so long that she's ready for anything and overly impressed with nobody.

When Karen is having a particularly rough day, she calls in reinforcements—and they're good reinforcements. A picture of St. Thérèse of Lisieux hangs where Karen can always see it, and "Tessie" is called on in fervent prayer whenever Karen needs special help. A picture of the Servant of God Cardinal Terence Cooke, along with a scrap of cloth from a shirt he once wore, is on her desk. If "Tessie" doesn't come through for Karen, "Cookie" certainly will. Did I mention that Karen is not overly impressed with anybody?

Karen has lived most of her life within a stone's throw of my office at Trinity Retreat in Larchmont, New York, and at one time she was the best-known person in town, recognized by everyone. Although unfailingly kind, she could—with a word or two—decisively put people in their place, which is not a bad quality for a receptionist to have. I tell her this proves she's a true Larchmonter.

At her desk Karen faces two large windows, and these windows give her a perfect view of Long Island Sound, which is literally a few feet away. It's a beautiful place to spend the workday. I look in on her sometimes, when she doesn't notice, especially during those times when the phone calls have abated for a while. She's gazing out at the sound, thinking, praying, just contemplating the way the sun glistens on the water, or watching the rain fall. At times I can tell she's absorbed in the slow movement of our pair of resident swans as they pass her windows. I've never asked, but I'm sure she's named every one of the many seabirds she sees. Then the phone suddenly rings; the reverie ends, and Karen swings into action.

Some people would call Karen disabled. They're the ones who've never met her. She calls herself "inconvenienced." But after you know her for a while, you begin to forget about her inconvenience; you almost don't see her ever-present wheelchair. She's extraordinary but so quietly so that you don't notice it. So many things that are easy for the rest of us are difficult for her, but you don't always see that. She makes the difficulties of her life seem to disappear.

Karen lives completely on her own in an apartment that's been remodeled to fit her short stature and allow for her inability to walk. The apartment is neat, clean, and welcoming. Like her desk, it's filled with pictures of animals but not just pictures! I said that Karen lives alone, but that's not quite true: She has two roommates.

One is Shadow, a large and somewhat temperamental African Gray parrot. The second roommate is Scamper, a gray cat that was found as a kitten in the Bronx and taken to Trinity Retreat. There it came every day to take a nap in Karen's wastepaper basket (which Karen always kept clean and empty so as not to disturb the kitten). From that point we all knew where this cat would end up, and so it did—happy, content, and much loved in Karen's home.

I think of the immense number of people over the last thirty-five years whom Karen has helped, encouraged, and prayed for. She's been a blessing to many and has hung up the phone on remarkably few.

But thirty-five years is a long time, and many things have changed. The book about Karen is out of print. She is no longer the best-known person in Larchmont. However, I know she is still one of the most respected and loved people who have ever lived in this beautiful little village on the shore of Long Island Sound.

CHAPTER EIGHTEEN

Fr. Bob Stanion

Fr. Robert Stanion, C.F.R., is without a doubt one of the most colorful characters and kindly people whom I have ever met. His death in March of 2009 was mourned by thousands of people in Boston, in the New York area, and especially in Albuquerque, New Mexico, where he lived and worked the last years of his life.

There are innumerable stories about Fr. Bob. He was the sort of person who seemed to generate stories without ever trying. All of these tales are interesting, many of them are rather moving, and quite a few of them are unexpectedly humorous. One might say that characters like Fr. Bob aren't very common in our contemporary world; his type of warm-hearted and generous eccentricity seemed to come from at least a hundred years before.

Born in 1947, Fr. Bob grew up in Summerville, Massachusetts. When he was eighteen he entered religious life, becoming a postulant in the Capuchin order, and as Br. Vianney he became a fully professed brother at the age of twenty-five. He was among the first Franciscan Friars of the Renewal when we formed our new community in 1987. He was ordained to the priesthood in 1992.

Those are rather dry facts, and they don't really tell you much about the fascinating and engaging person who was Fr. Bob Stanion. He was a deeply religious man, and I would say that faith came very naturally to him. In fact, I think it is accurate to say that he had the great gift of a faith virtually untroubled by doubt. This powerful faith was what enabled him to face life with what the French like to call *joie de vivre*. He loved being with people; in fact, he loved doing all sorts of things.

Among his many talents (and things he took to be his talents) was cooking. Fr. Bob loved the kitchen; for him it was a laboratory in which he could experiment to his heart's content. He was the great master of the low-budget gourmet meal and specialized in a rather idiosyncratic version of Chinese food. Nothing edible could escape his experimentation; he cooked, pickled, or canned virtually anything that couldn't outrun him, including things that he lovingly grew each summer in his own garden. His spice rack was legendary, containing both the common and the esoteric. Many of those jars were filled with herbs he had grown and dried and spices that he had painstakingly ground into fine powders.

Fr. Bob so rarely became angry that some people thought that he wasn't even capable of anger. These people were obviously absent the day he discovered that some well-meaning person had "weeded" his garden, uprooting and discarding all his beloved herbs (which really did look like weeds).

Before his ordination Br. Bob was for several years the cook at Trinity Retreat House, where I have lived since 1974. Trinity primarily serves the clergy, and it was not unusual to have members of the hierarchy visit. Today such visits generally pose few problems, but during Br. Bob's tenure at Trinity, things were very different.

Soon after his arrival I learned that such visits were destined to be moments of high anxiety for me. To say that Br. Bob was somewhat lacking in a sense of formality around the hierarchy is a gross understatement. I'll never forget exactly how

I felt the day he greeted Cardinal Cooke at the door with a hearty "Welcome to Trinity, Your Em-and-Ems!" Of course, this was only the beginning; he spent the rest of the day calling the cardinal "Your Insignificance" and the hierarchy the "lowerarchy."

Luckily, if there was a kinder man than Br. Bob in the whole archdiocese of New York, it was Cardinal Cooke. He took all this with great good humor. That fact did not prevent me from spending much of that day looking for places to hide Br. Bob should any other prelate decide to darken our door.

From his days as a young brother—and possibly before—Fr. Bob struggled with illness and infirmity. Most people were unaware of this, as he rarely spoke about his difficulties. It was not unusual for him to find his life interrupted in one way or another by problems with his back or neck. Various unexpected and seemingly unrelated illnesses would also affect him over and over again. Such problems did not seem to fit with the vivacious personality of this man, but he always took them in stride and usually rebounded from them quickly.

Finally, however, doctors told Fr. Bob that because of his back and neck conditions, a fall might permanently cripple him. For this and other reasons, he was advised to leave the northeast, with its treacherous ice and snow, and relocate in a warmer, gentler climate. So off to Albuquerque went Fr. Bob. There he became a pioneer of the Franciscans of the Renewal and, true to form, developed a large and devoted group of friends. Although he came to the priesthood late, he was a priest through and through and did much good for many people in the Southwest.

Even there, however, his physical problems began to mount, until finally three threatening illness converged on him, presenting him with the greatest challenge to his health thus far. It is very typical of him that, even as he faced this new crisis, he remained very involved in working with three men, each of whom suffered some life-threatening illness. Each received his special interest, care, and constant prayers.

It soon became clear that this time Fr. Bob would not rebound from his illnesses. The time was approaching for him to go home to God. His health steadily worsened until he was in the hospital, virtually immobile and in great suffering. From our point of view, it seems tragic that such a vivacious person could so quickly be reduced to a complete invalid. It is disturbing for us and shows something we prefer to ignore, that human life is terribly fragile, that the future is never a sure thing in this passing world.

Fr. Bob spent the next several weeks immobile and unable to communicate. He seemed to hover between this world and the next. Finally death came, releasing him.

Fr. Bob was no less different from other people in death than he had been in life: He had two funerals, one in New York and the other in Albuquerque. Each was a celebration of the life of a man beloved by many. His memorial card includes this quotation from the great Dom Helder Camara, a Brazilian archbishop and great apostle: "Say yes to the surprises which interrupt your plans and crush your dreams, giving your day—perhaps your life—a completely new direction." I can't think of a more fitting quotation for Fr. Bob.

Those who knew Fr. Bob and truly appreciate the beautiful Catholic theologies of death and eternal life pray in hope and joy for the soul of this very good man as he makes his journey to God. *Purgatory* is a frightening word for most Catholics, but it shouldn't be. Pope Benedict himself has suggested an alternative name, one that should cause no fear: "the intermediate state between death and resurrection."[1] It is here that my good friend Fr. Bob is, I believe, being made ready for his everlasting encounter with the Holy Trinity.

As one who looks forward to purgatory, I strongly suspect that the presence of Fr. Bob will have a salutary effect on the place. Since his arrival I'm sure there's been a great deal more laughter. And you never know, maybe they're even getting some good, low-cost, gourmet Chinese food.

CHAPTER NINETEEN

Mother Angelica

I was in England. It was a busy afternoon, and I was devoting myself to a thousand things when the phone rang. I picked it up almost absentmindedly, and almost before I could say hello, a sharp voice rang in my ear. "I've already made eight calls trying to find you, and now I've finally tracked you down in England. Anyway, I want to get you on our program."

I had no idea who was calling, although the voice was certainly American and not English. Was this a wrong number or perhaps a crank call? For a second or two I was tempted to hang up. The voice continued speaking as I tried to decide what to do, and slowly it began to dawn on me: This was Mother Angelica. She was not well-known at that time, a woman whose name I had heard but whom I had never met.

Thus began a relationship that has lasted for twenty-five years.

My first visit to EWTN occurred not long after this phone call, and it was nothing short of astonishing. The convent of the cloistered Poor Clares of Perpetual Adoration was attached to the television studio, and compared to the way things are now, it was very primitive. Nevertheless, Mother was moving full steam ahead. At that point she was ready to go full-time with her broadcasting, and EWTN was on the verge of becoming the largest religious television network in the entire world. A network started by a cloistered Franciscan nun! As we say in Jersey City, "Go figure!"

As is the case with many of the people I'm writing about in this book, it's not necessary to give a biography of Mother Angelica. This has been done quite well by Raymond Arroyo, who has been a mainstay of EWTN for years and is a good friend of Mother. But as anyone who has ever seen Mother Angelica on television surely knows, there is no shortage of colorful stories that I could tell regarding her. Here I want to limit myself to a couple of anecdotes and some reflections.

The first thing I noticed when I met this remarkable person was that she was a superb communicator. In fact, I have to say that she was probably the best untrained communicator I have ever met. In Mother Angelica's case, there was no such thing as wasted words: What was on her mind was also on her lips. Whether she was speaking of her own ideas or trying to find out about your ideas, she was not the sort of person who had to work to figure out what she wanted to say. The words were always there for her, and they were usually insightful, always to the point, and often remarkably entertaining.

Mother Angelica had a simple goal that hasn't changed over many years: to inject Catholic devotion into the often barren and usually pagan world of television. In pursuing this goal she was single-minded: She never looked to the right or the left, and she certainly never looked behind in regret. She simply looked forward, firm in her ideas, determined to claim at least one corner of the vast wasteland we call television for Christ.

She did this despite the fact that she was well aware that she couldn't count on support from everyone and that there were a number of groups in the Catholic community whose points of view differed greatly from her own. She certainly knew that not everybody liked all of her presentations. Did this bother

her very much? Of course not. She carried on, trusting in God and doing her best.

I've always thought that Mother Angelica arrived on the scene at precisely the right moment. As we look back over the seventies, it seems that we in the Church were dedicating ourselves too much to being part of the "American pie." Everybody was getting along with everybody. Differences were being politely swept under any available rug. The issues of abortion and euthanasia were certainly there, but they had not yet become as divisive as they presently are. There was also a rather sharp distinction then between liberal and conservative Catholics, which has blurred over time, but things had not yet become bitter. It was into this world of somewhat forced pleasantness and superficial papering over of differences that Mother Angelica injected herself. The world hasn't been quite the same since.

Many people tend to think of nuns as shy and retiring. The same people think of cloistered nuns as being absolutely out of touch with reality, of having retreated into the cloister because they couldn't deal with the world. One hour with Mother Angelica is all it would take to disabuse anyone of such foolish notions.

I recall that famous evening when Mother was very annoyed by some public statements made on behalf of the American hierarchy. These were made not by the bishops themselves but by public relations people whom they employed. Mother was not amused, and she set things straight on the air, mincing no words. Such behavior was typical of this fighter, whose patron saint sometimes seemed to be Joan of Arc rather than Clare of Assisi.

One evening I was at EWTN when she talked on television for half an hour straight. She sat there with nothing written in front of her, nothing prepared, and very eloquently and powerfully threw down the gauntlet before "liberal Catholicism." Let me tell you, this was an apocalyptic speech if ever there was one. I believe that it was at that moment that Mother Angelica emerged as a force to be reckoned with.

There are various people who attempted to get her out of the public scene. Hers was not the smiley-faced brand of Catholicism that was then in vogue, and she was seen by some as a hindrance to ecumenism. But hindsight shows us that she was right. Many of the Protestant bodies with whom we were trying to improve our relationship were quick to part company with us over abortion, euthanasia, same-sex marriage, the ordination of people involved in same-sex relationships, and a host of other issues. Little of this had happened when Mother began broadcasting, but the winds of change were blowing, and it seemed that she was among the few who felt them.

I remember sitting in an auditorium at Mundelein Seminary. A large collection of Catholic religious, particularly sisters of traditional communities, had gathered under the chairmanship of Fr. John Hardon, S.J., a devout, very intelligent man who had made a profound contribution to establishing relationships between religious communities. This meeting would contribute to the formation of the Council of Major Superiors of Women Religious.

Mother Angelica entered the room and told us (for what reason I will never understand) that the sisters who had taught her were crabby, that she managed to get thrown out of Catholic school three times, and that she only got back in twice. Then she took off like a rocket. That day she actually said, "Before I allow the USCC [United States Catholic Conference] to take over EWTN, I'll blow up the whole damn thing." As she uttered these words for all to hear, I watched Fr. Hardon turn to white marble before my eyes. I, on the other hand, nearly had to be carried out of the room and given artificial respiration on the lawn from laughing so hard. But that was Mother Angelica in rare and wonderful form.

A totally different picture of this fascinating and unusual woman is emerging as she approaches the end of her life. At the time I am writing these words, Mother Angelica has experienced several severe strokes. She can hardly talk, and she cannot stand. Some time ago I was at her convent, talking to the sisters at the grille. Knowing Mother was never one to beat around the bush, I said to her very directly, "Mother, I believe you're the greatest natural communicator I've ever known, and it must be very hard for you not to be able to speak."

She was smiling, but then a dark moment of sorrow came over her face. I felt I had said exactly the wrong thing, but then the dark look disappeared as quickly as it had appeared. It was almost like a windshield wiper removing rain. As I thought about it later, I realized that Mother Angelica did not want me to see her suffering. She did not want her suffering to cause me pain.

Mother continues to suffer—no one of us can imagine how much, but I am sure her suffering is great at times. I am also sure she has made of that suffering a beautiful offering to God. It is suffering transformed into prayer, and I believe it plays a large part in causing EWTN to continue to be the incredible experience it is for millions of people, not only in the United States but in Europe, Latin America, and even Asia. In many places in the world, even in places in which few people speak English, people have come up to me and told me they've seen me on EWTN. None of this would have happened without Mother Angelica. EWTN wouldn't have happened without Mother Angelica

Solid catechesis has been lacking in many places for many years now. This has produced a Catholic population that knows little of the truths of the faith. Mother Angelica, however, the great communicator of the Church in America, has been a powerful force against lukewarm, incomplete, and erroneous teaching. Uncompromisingly, twenty-four hours a day, she taught the truths of the Church over ETWN.

It is impossible to estimate all that has been accomplished through the faith, prayerfulness, and courage of a cloistered nun in a poor convent in a very Protestant part of the country. Who among us is ready to deny that this is a work of God?

CHAPTER TWENTY

Liberal and Conservative Together in Faith:
Fr. George Barry Ford and Fr. John Anthony Hardon, S.J.

As I prepared to write this section of *Travelers Along the Way*, I must admit that a certain amount of anxiety accompanied the decision to combine Fr. Ford and Fr. Hardon in one chapter. Fr. Ford, as many of my older readers will remember, was very well-known in New York. For many years he was the legendary pastor of Corpus Christi Church. He was also, by the way, considered to be one of the great liberals of the city—and in New York there's a lot of stiff competition for titles like that. This, of course, was many years ago, before the Second Vatican Council and before the tumultuous political world of the sixties and beyond transformed the meaning of the words *liberal* and *conservative*, perhaps beyond recognition.

Fr. Hardon, on the other hand, was a wonderful Jesuit and a prolific author. He was also well-known, and the many people who knew him considered him to be the great conservative voice of the Church in New York (and a few other places as well). Fr. Hardon was a powerful supporter of traditional Catholicism, a man whose faith was utterly unaffected by trends or fashions. He was a brilliant and thoughtful man, and he was a conservative to the very depths of his soul.

Why in the world did I decide to put these two together? you might ask. Well, as I said, it wasn't an easy decision. But I'm beginning to think that I'm the only one left who knew the two of them fairly well, and I can say that despite their many obvious differences, both men shared a great deal of common ground.

Very explicitly, despite their differing viewpoints, they came together in their complete acceptance of the teachings of the Catholic Church. No one who ever knew him could accuse Fr. Ford of departing from the teachings of the Church in any way. The exact same thing could be said of Fr. Hardon—who has from time to time been called more Roman than the pope.

And here we find something important: a realization that God, faith in God, and faith in God's Church have nothing whatsoever to do with the fashions of the moment. They involve no ideology; they do not depend on how we perceive things in this passing world. God and our faith in God transcend such things. Conservatism and liberalism—however we define them—may be lenses through which we perceive the world, but we cannot and must not use such lenses to perceive the God who transcends the world and all human categories. Neither Fr. Ford nor Fr. Hardon ever would.

But now let us take a brief look at each of these two remarkable men.

Fr. George Barry Ford was born in the small upstate city of Ithaca, known primarily as the location of Cornell University, and was ordained for the archdiocese of New York. For many years he was utterly devoted to the poor of the city, and he worked very successfully and diligently among them. The stories of his caring for the poor are legion, yet if you didn't know him, you'd think him very out of place in such work. A well-dressed, impeccably groomed, and very proper man, Fr. Ford at times seemed almost patrician when he was surrounded by New York City's poor. But I doubt that he ever thought of himself in that way. He was always very outgoing and friendly to all who approached him and genuinely concerned about those whom society overlooked. He was a very formal man, as many of his generation (those born at the end of the nineteenth century) were. Fr. Ford always wore clerical attire and was absolutely shocked to learn soon before his death that some priests were actually appearing in public without their Roman collars.

He was appointed chaplain of Columbia University, where he did very good work, and then, in 1934, he began his long pastorate of Corpus Christi Church, which was only a couple of blocks from the north end of the campus. His progressivism was demonstrated by a strong concern for education. This resulted in his building (during the Depression) a beautiful combination school and church.

The school, by the way, was for years studied, discussed, and imitated by others throughout the country. It was operated by the Dominican Sisters of Sinsinawa, and everyone knew it was of the highest quality. It had among its faculty lay teachers who were trained in secular universities—a very daring move at the time. At various points the school even abolished grades.

Fr. Ford showed his liberalism in other ways as well. He once encouraged striking workers from Consolidated Edison (New York's electrical power company) to use rooms in his school for meetings. I suspect this decision did nothing to endear him to the heart of Cardinal Francis Spellman, then New York's archbishop.

Fr. Ford's church, along with his school, was considered unusual and innovative in its style. Corpus Christi was done in a rather classical design, mixing English and American motifs. It is interesting to look at that church now, in light of what we have called "progressive" in the last few decades. It is light-years away from the sometimes bizarre and outright ugly innovations of modern church architecture. Corpus Christi certainly cannot be called ornate; it is instead quietly beautiful in its decoration, simple but very different from the stark and virtually empty "worship spaces" that became all the rage about twenty years ago. Many people, including the Trappist monk Thomas Merton, compared it to the oratory of Philip Neri.

Fr. Ford was very much a supporter of the arts, and he created a unique music program at Corpus Christi, one that—amazingly—continues to this very day. When Fr. Ford introduced it, it seemed shockingly different from the music in most Catholic churches. It seems even more radically different today. At Corpus Christi one hears beautiful and dignified music offered solemnly for the glory of God. The great music that has been written for the Church over many centuries forms the basis of the music there, and Gregorian chant is given pride of place.

Solemnity, a reserved beauty, and a kind of timelessness are the hallmarks of the music Fr. Ford chose. He had absolutely no interest in any kind of popular religious music and would have been appalled at the "hootenanny" liturgies that became popular in the sixties and beyond. I think if a guitar should ever be strummed in the sanctuary of his church, he would rise from his grave, grab the offending instrument, and bash it over the head of the musician—but only in the most gentlemanly of ways.

The combination of beautiful liturgy, the great musical heritage of the Church, and the cosmopolitan nature of Fr. Ford attracted many from the intellectual community that lived around Columbia University, and more than a few of them entered the Church at the baptismal font at Corpus Christi.

Thomas Merton is only the most famous of those whom Fr. Ford introduced to the Church. Interestingly Fr. Ford served for a time as a spiritual advisor to Eleanor Roosevelt. She even called for him at the time of her death, but the Roosevelt family did not honor this request, and Fr. Ford was not able to see her.

I find it very interesting that this great liberal of only a few years ago would now be seen by many Catholics as a conservative. Fr. Ford's love of liturgy and insistence that God is best worshiped with dignity and solemnity would make him sadly out of step with our own time, which unfortunately is characterized by liturgies that seem so casual that they sometimes manage to obscure the holiness of the Mass.

On the other side of the liberal-conservative divide stands Fr. John Hardon. Younger than Fr. Ford, he was born in 1914 to a very devout Catholic family. He entered the Society of Jesus and was ordained in 1947. In those days the Jesuits were the great defenders of orthodox Catholicism, although today at times they seem to have become something different.

Fr. Hardon studied at John Carroll University and obtained his doctorate from the Gregorian University in Rome with a dissertation on the papacy. While in Rome at the Gregorian, one of the librarians asked young Fr. Hardon to retrieve a number of books. Always curious, he began to examine these books, and he found to his chagrin that at least some espoused doctrines that he considered not truly Catholic. He wrote, "Before I had retrieved one half of the heretical books I had become an agent of orthodoxy and therefore the sworn enemy of modernists, who were updating the Catholic faith to its modernist theology. I had doors slammed in my face. I lost friends I had considered believers."[1]

Thus began the career of a defender of orthodoxy, and throughout the many long years of his life, Fr. Hardon never ceased in that struggle. In fact, for many people it seemed to define this wonderful priest. Despite his numerous and varied accomplishments, Fr. Hardon remained known up to the very time of his death primarily as one of the great defenders of orthodoxy. This was not always easy for him. In some ways it actually distanced him from the religious order of which he was a part. In the decades after the Second Vatican Council, the Jesuits went through many changes, not all of them good ones, and Fr. Hardon sometimes found himself marginalized in his own community.

I attended Fr. Hardon's funeral, and I can say that many of the Jesuits there did not seem to understand or appreciate him. Perhaps they, liberals in the current sense of the word, could not comprehend his conservatism; they couldn't look beyond their own ideas and categories to the fundamental things they shared with Fr. Hardon. At times during the eulogy I sensed what seemed to be a subtle scorn; in any event I don't think Fr. Hardon received the eulogy he deserved, and in my own small way, I have tried whenever possible to remind people of the importance and dedication of this wonderful Jesuit.

Like Fr. Ford, Fr. Hardon's commitment to Christ and to the Church transcended anything that could be called conservatism. He included among his close friends Mother Teresa and others who were simply above such distinctions. They saw people not as liberals or conservatives but only as children of God, made in the divine image.

Fr. Hardon was responsible for a number of books on the faith geared to the lay reader. He had an extraordinary gift for explaining the Church to those who were confused by or unaware of Catholic teachings. His *Catholic Catechism,* published in 1975, was an extremely important book in the perplexing days following the Second Vatican Council. There he clearly and dispassionately explains the Church's position on many topics that have been distorted by others.

Later, in 1980, he published *The Modern Catholic Dictionary,* another fine book. Some years later he was a consultant for the official *Catechism of the Catholic Church,* written primarily by Cardinal Schönborn of Austria.

Basically Fr. Hardon was a catechist. Although I suspect that as a young man he expected to spend his life teaching in a university or focusing on very narrow theological questions, he did neither of these things because he saw a greater need. Instead he taught the Catholic faith to as many people as possible. Through his books and other works, he taught generations of people the essentials of the faith during a time when such things seemed to be up for grabs. In my opinion he is one of the great evangelists of the modern world.

I had the opportunity to know both Fr. Hardon and Fr. Ford fairly well, but as far as I know, they never met. I can't say for sure what would have happened if I had introduced them to each other, but I suspect these very proper and highly intelligent priests would have managed to get along quite well.

This pair of priests show us how little the words *conservative* and *liberal* mean in the world of religion. These words, which come from politics, show our contemporary confusion as to what constitutes real religion. When we apply them to the world of faith, we show how little we know. *Conservative* means "dedicated to keeping the status quo." Does this word define a man like Fr. Hardon, who wanted the status quo to change immediately and in the right direction?

If you had asked Fr. Ford about liberals, he probably would have told you that the word really means having respect for someone you disagree with. Fr. Ford always had such respect. He would be totally opposed to today's liberals who seem to have no patience with anyone who holds ideas contrary to their own.

Of course, these men lived in different times. Fr. Ford was very much a man before the council, and Fr. Hardon very much one after it. Fr. Hardon was often disturbed by the sloppy and even heretical versions of Catholicism that developed in his own backyard—and in his own religious community. Fr. Ford would have been just as shocked if he had lived to witness such developments. Both men were completely dedicated to the Catholic faith.

If you could put these two great men together in the present situation, I wonder what they would say to each other. If such conversations can be held after this life, I hope that my two good friends will one day invite me to such a talk. It'll be a good discussion: Each will have his own opinion, but their opinions will be much closer than they would have appeared in this world.

Much can be learned from these two men, especially the unity of commitment to the Christian life and the Catholic faith. I can imagine Fr. Hardon concelebrating Mass with Fr. Ford and preaching in Corpus Christi Church. If such an event could ever have happened, we would have seen a great liberal and a great conservative together at the altar of Christ, but far more importantly, we would have seen two great priests absolutely united in their love of Christ and His Church.

CHAPTER TWENTY-ONE

Fr. Isidore Kennedy

As soon as I arrived at the Santa Inez Friary in California, I was met by my classmate, Fr. Marian, who was then novice master of this Irish province of the Capuchins in the far West. I could see right away that he was excited, and I suspected this might not be due entirely to the fact that I had arrived to give the friars a retreat. It didn't take long for me to discover the reason, however, for he greeted me with "Oh, we have a saint!"

I didn't miss a beat. My response was "Oh, delightful. I love to watch saints. Luckily, I brought my saint-evaluation questionnaire with me." With that we entered the friary.

My friend explained that Father (the saintly one) would not be there until the next day, and that I would be able to meet him when he came to lunch. I decided that my only course of action was to wait with bated breath until the appointed time.

The next day, as soon as I entered the refectory, I surveyed the room and discovered that it was not particularly difficult to pick this saint out. He looked the part. He was tall, thin, and elderly, with a white beard in the Capuchin style and an absolutely cherubic smile. I was very pleased to see that the friars had arranged for me to sit next to him after the reading of the gospel.

Afterward, as we began to eat lunch, I mentioned that he'd been away the day before. He nodded and then, in a lilting Irish accent, responded, "Oh, I just got out of the hospital. I was only there for six weeks, and it was lovely, because hospitals have improved so much over the years."

I decided to ask him how often he'd been in the hospital. To that he cheerfully responded, "Sixty-six times since I was seventeen years old."

Somewhat astonished at this, I asked, "Well, what was your longest stay in the hospital?"

Without an instant's hesitation he responded, "Four and a half years in the sanatorium in Arizona. Oh, it was lovely. Every evening they used to push us out onto a flat roof, and I watched the stars—every night. It was quite lovely. It never rains there, you know. It was grand."

I was beginning to doubt whether all of this was on the up-and-up. Surely something about this had to be a put on. But this man seemed to be so utterly simple and sincere that I couldn't be sure.

He proceeded to explain to me that he had been sent from Ireland to the United States many years before as a very young brother. He was expected at the time to die shortly of tuberculosis, but it was thought that the Southwestern climate might buy him a little time. In fact, he managed to outlive everyone who had sent him to the United States, most of them by a good number of years.

"Really?" I said as he told me this. And looking slightly pleased with himself, he reminded me that the Irish have a saying, "Only the good die young."

Well, I spent a week sitting next to Fr. Isidore (for that was his name), and that week turned out to be a delightful adventure. I never quite knew from a conversation's beginning where it would wind up. He was a man who had a very different way of looking at the world from that of most other people. Apparently he looked down at it from up in the sky.

I learned that much of his life had consisted of a series of lonely assignments in remote mission parishes in the far West. Usually this would involve a few people coming to a tiny chapel with a little three- or four-room rectory. These had been built mostly by the Catholic Extension Society and were not uncommon in the area.

From time to time the provincial would make a visit to Fr. Isidore at one of these remote missions. He'd make the journey by train, and when he arrived he'd usually discover that the rectory was filled with some of the homeless women who seemed to be as common as tumbleweeds in the area. The homeless men, along with Fr. Isidore, could be found sleeping on the benches of the little church each night. When visiting Fr. Isidore, the provincial never knew what to expect—except for one thing: Fr. Isidore would be broke. He had no ability whatsoever to manage money, and he spent whatever meager funds came his way buying food and other necessities for the poor. There was usually nothing left over for himself, but such things were not of any particular concern to Fr. Isidore.

After several years of this remarkable missionary endeavor, something like a sense of guilt caused the superiors of the order to appoint Fr. Isidore pastor of a normal-size parish in a more inhabited area. He dutifully went and lasted exactly six months. In other words, that was the length of time it took him to give absolutely everything away. Unsurprisingly he found himself back in Gopher Gulch or Willow Creek, or wherever the superiors thought that Fr. Isidore could do the least amount of financial damage. As a result, he spent the vast majority of his life as a kind of informal Capuchin-Franciscan hermit—something of a rarity.

Time wore on until one day someone realized that Fr. Isidore was getting on in years. It was decided that he should retire, and Father was moved from his lonely existence in the boondocks into the novitiate, where he was to spend most of the rest of his life (when he was not in the hospital, that is). This afforded me the opportunity to observe this unusual man on my excursion to the West. And there was a lot to observe, especially when it came to his prayer life.

The younger brothers at that time referred to Fr. Isidore's daily private prayer as "Izzy's trip," an expression derived from the psychedelic "trips" that were a popular and illegal pastime during the period. He spent from one o'clock to five every day in the chapel sitting before the Blessed Sacrament. During these periods he seemed all but oblivious of anything that might be going on, and he spent this lengthy time sitting ramrod straight with his eyes gently closed. I once sat behind him and observed that his back never even touched the bench on which he was sitting. Even from a distance of only a foot or two, it was strangely difficult to discern whether he was actually breathing.

The brothers all knew that if there was some work going on near the chapel during these times, if someone should be hammering or making some other noise, Fr. Isidore would be completely unaware of it. At times people would apologize to him for the noise they had to make, and he would always say, "Oh, I didn't hear that at all." Despite this, however, if it was his responsibility to respond to the doorbell, he would rise from his prayers as soon as it rang and warmly welcome whatever guest was at the door.

For some reason—as in the case of Fr. Solanus—people did not seem to appreciate the remarkable holiness of this man. In fact, in the case of Fr. Isidore, there was at times a subtle ridicule. For instance, since Fr. Isidore always wore an old-fashioned pair of spectacles that were perfectly round, he was known quietly as "the Jeep," because Jeeps used to have perfectly round headlights

I was finishing up my week in California and hoping I might get a further opportunity to look into the life of this remarkable man. I got my chance when he actually came to me for confession. Of course, I can never tell anything that I have heard in the confessional, and I would never desire to do so anyway. However, if I were ever to be so tempted, it would probably be with Fr. Isidore's confession.

With the greatest humility Fr. Isidore knelt on the floor before this friar who was so much younger than he was and confessed what he considered to be his sins. I can say that his was a confession of great beauty and holiness. After I gave him absolution, I asked him to get off the floor and sit in a chair. I wanted to ask him some questions.

Slowly (and with a little help) he made it into the chair. Then I said to him, "Father, I noticed that you have a great sense of humor."

He seemed pleased at this, and his immediate response was, "My mother's people were the McDermotts, and they were famous for their love of a good joke."

Figuring the ice had been broken, I moved in to see what I could find out. "Father," I inquired, "you have a secret, don't you?"

Now, everyone knows that old Jewish people are justly famous for answering a question with a question; but let me tell you, they have nothing on the old Irish, who have even given a name to such behavior. It's called *knapping*, and Fr. Isidore proved to be a master of knapping. He looked at me calmly and in a quizzical-sounding voice asked, "A secret, do you say?"

I affirmed that I had indeed said he had a secret, and then Father said, "Well, it may be true. I might have a little secret."

Feeling I was making some kind of progress, I continued. "Could you please tell me what it is?"

To which he replied, "Well, if I tell you, then it wouldn't still be a secret, would it?"

At that point I began to suspect that I had just entered a maze of knapping. Deciding it was time for the direct approach, I said, "Father, I am very interested in the way people lead their spiritual lives, and I was wondering if you might share with me something of yours—perhaps a few insights. Could you please tell me this secret of yours?"

Seconds passed, so many that they seemed ready to add up to minutes, before he finally said in the most old-fashioned of Irish ways, "Well, it ain't much." And for a second I thought that was to be the end of things.

But doggedly I asked, "What's that?"

And then he said it: "Well, it's just a little something that comes to me every day, particularly when things are not quite up to the mark. It's sort of an imagination . . . or an experience. [The word *experience* is my interpretation.] During the day, when I stop to think about it, it seems to me that I've spent my whole life sitting in the place of St. John at the Last Supper."

I was astonished and greatly moved by these words spoken by this holy and humble man. I have read many books about contemplation and other spiritual states. I have never, however, even in the cases of the great mystics like St. Teresa of Ávila, read a more profound or succinct description of Christian contemplation. Here was a man hardly noticed by anyone who spent much of his life so spiritually aware that he understood, felt, and regularly experienced something that great saints rarely feel: the great love of Jesus for the beloved disciple at the Last Supper. If I hadn't realized it before, I now certainly knew I was in the presence of someone very special.

Years later I returned to Santa Inez. I walked along the side of the cloister until I came to a tiny cemetery. There, among the plain small granite markers, was one that simply said, "Father Isidore Kennedy, born in Drombain, County Tipperary, died at Santa Inez."

In the simple but holy life of Fr. Isidore, we are granted an important insight: Great saints may often not be recognized or even noticed by people during their earthly lives. The recognized saints are chosen by Divine Providence and proclaimed by the Church to give us public examples and encouragement, but it would be a very distorted and impoverished view of things to think they are alone. Right among us are people we never notice, people who are so close to God that they can regularly rest their heads on Jesus' breast, as did the beloved disciple at the Last Supper.

CHAPTER TWENTY-TWO

Judge William P. Clark

My first meeting with Judge Clark was one of those encounters you don't soon forget. It occurred outside the Westchester County prison on the day I was released from jail. I had been arrested in the town of Dobbs Ferry, New York, for the "crime" of saying the rosary in front of an abortion clinic. And so off to jail I went, where I found myself to be in very good company. I was arrested along with Bishop George Lynch and Br. Fidelis Moscinski, one of our friars who was then a seminarian and is now a priest.

I was released before either Br. Fidelis or the bishop, as this was my first incarceration, and the other two were already old hands at going to jail, having been arrested several times before for praying publicly for the unborn. Therefore I regained my freedom alone. When I came out onto the street, I discovered Judge Clark, standing with a number of friends. They had come to support and honor by their presence any pro-life people who were being released.

I was very pleased and also quite impressed. Here was a federal judge who had also been deputy secretary of state under President Reagan, secretary of the interior, and even national security advisor, one of the most important positions in the government. It is my strong suspicion that people with such resumes don't usually spend a lot of time in front of jails, greeting the newly sprung. I'm glad Judge Clark was an exception to this rule.

As I got to know him, I became more and more impressed with Judge Clark and came to the conclusion that he is not just an exemplary Catholic (which he is) but one of the true Catholic heroes of our time. A Californian by birth, he was educated at Stanford University and then Loyola Law School. Throughout his long and distinguished career, his faith has been his guide as well as his source of strength.

In time I came to realize there was more to him than just a public figure: He's the original family man. He and his wife, Joan, are devoted to their five children, whom they brought up on a huge ranch near Paso Robles, California. No matter how demanding Bill Clark's career became, he always made time for his children, just as he made time for his faith. In his later years, when his children were grown and on their own, the judge devoted much of his time to the building of a very beautiful mission-style chapel on top of a hill between his ranch house and the highway. This chapel is a jewel and a fitting home for the Blessed Sacrament. It's become a place where priests in the area come to offer Mass on Sundays, both in English and in Spanish.

President Reagan relied on Judge Clark immensely for years, and it has even been said that Reagan brought the Cold War to an end principally with the assistance of Judge Clark. President Reagan's son Michael once declared that no one knew his father as well as did the judge, and Norman A. Bailey of the National Security Council, said, "He did more than any other individual to help the President change the course of history and put an end to an empire that was, indeed, the embodiment of evil."[1]

These are certainly high accolades; just as certainly they never turned Judge Clark's head. He is unfailingly modest and down-to-earth.

In Bill Clark we find a type of person that has sadly become a rarity in today's world: an outstanding example of a truly dedicated Christian and exemplary Catholic in public life. All too often we see supposed Catholics in public office ignoring or even publicly contravening the laws of the Church and even the basic laws of morality. Bill Clark proves that this does not have to be the case. During his years in government, I would say that no Catholic layman deserved more respect than Bill did. Even those who disagreed with him admired him.

It goes without saying that politics can be extraordinarily competitive and even very negative. Attacks are so frequent that they have become the norm. Animosity is often considered unavoidable. However, when all is said and done, Bill Clark never participated in any of this viciousness. He had few real detractors and even fewer enemies. President Jimmy Carter, the Democrat defeated by Ronald Reagan, said, "Bill Clark knew how to make friends—even Democrats—and I am proud to have been one of his friends."[2] Here we see the result of living the Catholic faith, of not leaving it behind when you go to work. Bill Clark proves that living a truly Catholic Christian life can transform our world, step by step.

One of my favorite memories of Bill Clark is of him in our beautiful chapel, preparing everything for Mass and praying very quietly, seeking the presence of Christ. This is very characteristic of Bill. No matter where you encounter him, even if you just visit him at his ranch and watch him go about his daily life, you are aware that he is in the presence of Christ. It has often been said that in the home of a real Christian, "Christ is the head of the house; He presides over every meal, and he participates in every conversation." That is a tall order, but I believe it to be true of the home of Bill and Joan Clark

We are only too used to prominent Catholics falling short of the mark. Some of those we would like to look up to disappoint us greatly; some even cause great scandal. But in the life of this modest man who accomplished so much, we find a model of what a true Catholic life lived by a devout layman can be. Judge Clark's faith permeates every aspect of his life. He reassures us that such a life is still possible and gives us something to live up to in a world of embarrassingly low standards.

He is a great man, and I am proud to know him, even if I did have to get arrested to meet him.

CHAPTER TWENTY-THREE

Art and Mary Wiser

Few Catholics have heard of the *Bruderhof,*[1] and this is unfortunate. I have known this group of devout Christians for years, and I see in their simple and dedicated lives a powerful yearning to follow Christ. I also see in them a model that many—both Christian and non-Christian—could follow, a model of peaceful coexistence and of respect for others. If more people lived as do the *Bruderhof,* the world would be a much better place, and it would be much closer to God.

The *Bruderhof* (which means "brotherhood" in German) was founded about one hundred years ago near Fulda, a town in southern Germany. Their roots, however, extend far back in history to the Hutterites and other Anabaptists. The members of this group take seriously the idea that Christians should live a common life; they do, in fact, all live together as a group, forming a village in which all the homes are attached. Each family has its own bedrooms and a kind of sitting room with a small kitchen and a place to eat breakfast and lunch. The main meal each day, however, is eaten together in a large, common refectory, in which the group also meets for daily prayer. Although they marry and have families, the *Bruderhof* are in many ways similar to Catholic religious communities.

Most Christians learning about a group like the *Bruderhof* would want to find out about their theology. We tend to place Christians on a theological scale ranging from Catholicism and Eastern Orthodoxy on one side to extreme

Protestantism on the other. The *Bruderhof*, however, frustrate such attempts: Their theological positions are neither involved nor complex and are based almost entirely on the group's approach to reading the Bible, especially the New Testament. The inspirations of each person are also of importance and taken into account in formulating religious positions. They have no theologians or philosophers, nor do they think they need any. Their approach to Christianity is as simple as it is sincere.

The *Bruderhof* find their Christian identity largely through prayer and work. They are particularly engaged in the creation of various objects out of wood, producing things ranging from medical and surgical items, such as braces, to toys for young children. All are handcrafted with precision, and many have a kind of simple elegance. This sort of work is their main source of support. They wear no distinctive clothes but dress as plainly as possible. The men usually wear denim work jackets, and the women dress in solid colors and wear kerchiefs. This plainness marks them as being different from the rest of us.

After all that I've just written, it will probably come as a surprise to most people that the *Bruderhof* enjoy a close friendship with the archdiocese of New York. How this came to be may seem mysterious. Yet such a friendship exists and has existed for many years. In fact, members of the *Bruderhof* attended important events at St. Patrick Cathedral as invited guests of Cardinal O'Connor, and for seven years the *Bruderhof* worked with the archdiocese on an official statement regarding purity.

When the pope came to New York, the *Bruderhof* were in St. Patrick Cathedral in their denim work jackets. They sat there in the sanctuary, plain and simple, surrounded by Orthodox and Protestant hierarchs dressed in their best ecclesiastical finery. It was a scene to be observed, and I must say I enjoyed observing it.

The reason this unusual Protestant group have become close to the Catholic Church can actually be explained quite easily: It is our common commitment to the pro-life cause, a commitment so profound that it easily transcends denominational differences. The members of the *Bruderhof* see human life as absolutely sacred.

Thus they are also pacifists. This made for an interesting relationship with Cardinal O'Connor, who was a retired admiral and had been head of the military chaplains of the Navy. Despite these differences, somehow or other, the *Bruderhof* and the cardinal never clashed; in fact, they got along splendidly. I suppose that this was ultimately based on the fact that both were striving to do the will of God in a world that often makes such an effort very difficult. It may also be because pacifists and those in the military have more in common than you may suspect: Both groups hate war and have every reason to hope that it will not occur, though their responses to this challenge may be very different.

I have always enjoyed my visits to Woodcrest, the *Bruderhof*'s village in Ulster County, New York. Such visits are always occasions of spiritual depth. This place is a little haven, a place of peace very much in contrast to the world we usually inhabit. If you can imagine a whole village of people who not only get along with each other but actually work at getting along with each other, a group comprised of people whose goal is to show each other real love and affection, then you have imagined the *Bruderhof*'s little village.

In their understanding "to get along," to truly love one another, means that correction and admonishment is sometimes necessary. It also means that it is just as necessary to accept such correction and admonishment from others. It is the *Bruderhof*'s firm goal to accept and love each person the way God made that person, with all of his or her strengths and weaknesses. This takes humility and love. In fact you can say that their only real law is the law of love. The beautiful idealism of the *Bruderhof* is something that I've always appreciated.

Their elder, Johann Christoph Arnold, is author of a book entitled *Sex, God and Marriage*, which he personally gave to Cardinal Ratzinger. Over the years this truly remarkable book has been used in many Catholic schools and programs, because it represents such a fine expression of the moral teachings of the Christian faith.

Art and Mary Wiser, good friends of mine for years, are perfect examples of the *Bruderhof*. I met this deeply devout couple long ago, and we became fast friends despite the fact that (as we immediately realized) we came from opposite ends of the ecclesiastical world. The Wisers were baptized into this movement in 1958, but their ideals had been similar to those of the *Bruderhof* long before.

Art was a longtime pacifist. He spent time during World War II both in a work camp and a prison, where the government interned him as a conscientious objector. Most of the people who read this book will not be very familiar with either the pacifist movement or conscientious objectors, for the simple reason that in recent years there have been relatively few pacifists around. During the youth of Art and Mary Wiser, however, there were many. Despite this it took no small amount of courage to take such a stand during the days of the Second World War.

Mary beautifully gave a sense of what the life of the *Bruderhof* consists of in the following words: "Yes, I know the peace that Jesus gives, but for me it is not the serene peace without times of struggle. Eberhard [the founder of the *Bruderhof*], in his *Inner Land*, in his chapter 'The Peace of God,' says the message of peace means the fighting task of conquering all lands, our inner life included, through the weapons of the Spirit and subjecting them to His Lordship."

As I said, neither Art nor Mary was born into the *Bruderhof*. They were both students at Cornell University when they met. Mary came from a fairly privileged background, and Art was an idealistic young man whose parents and family had grown up in India. The two seemed an unlikely pair, yet clearly they were meant for each other. Because they had access to a first-class education, they could have easily lived comfortable upper-middle-class lives, but they did not. Instead they sought greater riches.

After the Wisers were married, they lived a penniless life in what was called the Macedonia Co-op. This was an attempt at bringing together a group of like-minded people to live in a communal way. It was guided by the desire to live a very literal gospel life and inspired by the Christian writer C.S. Lewis, whose book *Mere Christianity* was used almost as a blueprint for life. All their lives the Wisers straddled two worlds: The first was a world that appeared radical, different, and countercultural. The second was very much centered on the solid, healthy joys of family life.

Mary and Art were brought together more intimately by their understanding of the Christian faith, an understanding that came after a profound conversion of most of the Macedonia Co-op members during a reading of the Gospel of Luke. In time the Macedonia Co-op, whose ideals were similar to those of the *Bruderhof*, was absorbed into the larger organization. Art and Mary happily went with it, dedicating themselves to their new group.

I've had many discussions with the Wisers, and in nearly all of them the theological and ecclesiastical differences between their understanding of Christianity and mine have been apparent. Yet their gentleness, acceptance, and devotion to Christ make these differences manageable. For example, as a Catholic, I find a church building to be of importance. This is a foreign thought to them. In the simple gospel approach of the *Bruderhof*, there is no felt need for a church building and no real sense of sacred space (as was common in the early Church). For them wherever the Spirit abides is sacred space, and often they meet for prayer outside under the trees or in other natural settings. They do have a "church house" where they pray, a locale that often changes, with the congregation going from one house to another.

During the initial days of the pro-life movement and in response to the atrocious decision of the United States Supreme Court in 1973 that opened the door to unlimited abortion on demand, dedicated pro-life people of different backgrounds came together. It is in this setting that I met the Wisers. Though a decade and a half older than I am, they became my very good friends. Ours was a friendship with few questions asked and fewer problems. I think I was able to understand them to some degree better than others because of the Franciscan tradition, which is one of simplicity and acceptance of poverty.

The Wisers and the *Bruderhof* in general have much to teach us. I think it is important for my readers (most of whom will be Catholics) to realize that, although the Holy Spirit works powerfully and constantly within our own Church, which extends in an unbroken way back to the time of the apostles, the Holy Spirit can work wherever He wills. And in the simple but intensely Christian life of the *Bruderhof* and the Wisers, I believe we see this working of the Spirit. Historically we are as different as possible from them, but spiritually we are deeply connected.

I will always remember the incredible sight of Art and Mary Wiser and the other members of the *Bruderhof*, dressed in their simple way, standing with the dignitaries of many churches under the vaulted ceilings of St. Patrick Cathedral during a Solemn Pontifical Mass. Their blue denim and work jackets spoke of Christianity at least as eloquently as the magnificent robes of any archbishop.

CHAPTER TWENTY-FOUR

Cardinal John O'Connor

It's not easy to write about a man like Cardinal John O'Connor. In some ways he seems larger than life. He's also been written about a thousand times before—adored by many and vilified by some. For years, as archbishop of New York, he seemed almost the voice of the Church in the United States. He was a man who took things seriously and did the best he could.

In terms of personality he was vastly different from his predecessor, Cardinal Terence Cooke, yet at the end of life there came to be a strange similarity between the two. Each faced death in the way a Catholic Christian should, with courage and trust and unshakable hope. It has been said about Cardinal Cooke that he taught us how to die. In case we needed a refresher course, we certainly found one in Cardinal O'Connor's holy and brave death from cancer. Such people show us what true strength and true faith really are. We should be thankful for them.

But before he ever fell ill, Cardinal John O'Connor lived a full and vibrant life, a life filled with energy and accomplishment. I first met him when he came to Trinity Retreat House in Larchmont to spend a quiet, prayerful week. This was long before he was named archbishop of New York; in fact, he hadn't yet been consecrated a bishop. He was, however, already a leader: a rear admiral and the highest-ranking chaplain in the United States Navy.

I could tell as soon as I met him that he was serious and impressive, a man who commanded respect automatically and without really trying. But there was more to him than that. He had, I noticed, a kind of simplicity and also a certain air of irony with regard to himself. In short, he seemed to be careful not to be too impressed with himself.

It wasn't much later that John O'Connor retired from the Navy and was consecrated a bishop. Because of his background he was assigned as an auxiliary bishop for the military ordinariate, which at that time was headed by the archbishop of New York, Cardinal Terence Cooke. So John O'Connor, a Philadelphian, found himself in New York.

He immediately stood out. I remember an observant priest saying about him at that time, "This is a man who's not going to be an auxiliary bishop for the rest of his life." This seemed an odd remark to me, as I always hold all bishops in respect, whether auxiliaries or local ordinaries. Later on I thought about these words and realized that this priest was recognizing the real leadership qualities of John O'Connor.

Within a year of the time that John O'Connor was consecrated a bishop, the great Catholic apologist Frank Sheed died. Sheed had made an immense gift to Catholic life over many years, particularly through the many books he wrote and those he published through his company, Sheed and Ward. His death was a great loss.

Cardinal Cooke offered his funeral Mass, and—to my dismay—only one other bishop showed up. It was John O'Connor. I later asked him why he had come, and I was impressed with his reply: "Because I belong to the Catholic Evidence Guild."

Frank and his wife Maisie Ward were very prominent in the Catholic Evidence Guild and through it did immense service to the Church. This organization of Catholic laypeople who spread knowledge of the Catholic faith by distributing literature and even giving sidewalk talks and little pitches in the park was an important part of my life. I was pleased to see it meant a lot to Bishop O'Connor as well. I found it interesting to picture him as a young seminarian preaching the truths of the Church to passersby on the sidewalks in Philadelphia. I imagine he did it with intensity and honesty.

In the spring of 1983, John O'Connor was named bishop of Scranton, Pennsylvania, and I assumed he had left New York for good. I was very wrong. In October of that year, Cardinal Cooke died, and John O'Connor was brought from the diocese of Scranton right back to the archdiocese of New York, this time as its archbishop. This was a change! As I said, his was a totally different style from that of the gentle and almost self-effacing Cardinal Cooke.

Within a few days the city of New York was well aware that things were about to be very different at St. Patrick Cathedral. It took people a while to get used to Cardinal O'Connor, who could be—to put it mildly—very direct. However, he could also be very understanding and filled with compassion and not just for those who agreed with him; he was often surprisingly sensitive to the needs and feelings of even those who opposed him.

I remember an instance in which a well-known liberal political leader ran into bad times as a result of one of the many nasty political skirmishes that go on in New York. She was attacked in the newspapers—and let me tell you, you don't know what being attacked is until you've been attacked by the

New York media! Shortly after her embarrassment began, her home phone rang one evening. It was Cardinal O'Connor, whom she hardly knew but regularly disagreed with.

There he was on the phone reassuring her and telling her not to be discouraged, that the problems she was enduring were all part of a life in politics. "Stay around," he said. "You'll get another chance at making a difference." And she did stay around, perhaps because of the cardinal's encouragement.

Almost no one knew about this until Cardinal O'Connor died. At that point the woman wrote in *The New York Times* about the incident, admitting that she and the cardinal had regularly been on opposite sides of a number of issues, some of them relating to Catholic teaching. This Jewish and largely secular politician was very concerned that people know of the cardinal's kindness to her. She wanted people to understand what kind of man Cardinal O'Connor really was.

Bishops must submit their resignations to the Vatican when they reach their seventy-fifth birthday, and Cardinal O'Connor, of course, complied with this rule. Because of the onset of terminal cancer at around that time, however, he was allowed to stay on. I suppose those who knew of his situation expected him to fade slowly away. If that was the case, they certainly didn't know John O'Connor. He kept going at full speed, as if nothing was wrong.

Eventually, however, it became clear that illness was beginning to take its toll. During this time an important fundraising dinner was on the horizon, and he said to me, "You know, we have a big event coming up, and we desperately need it to make money for our Catholic schools. Pray for me that I'll be able to get through it."

This dinner has been sponsored for many years by an organization known as the Inner-City Scholarship Fund. Almost all the members of this organization are Jewish businessmen, which may seem odd, considering the fact that they give large sums of money to support Catholic schools. It's not so odd, however, if you know the story behind the founding of the Inner-City Scholarship Fund many years ago, during the time when Cardinal Spellman was archbishop of New York.

Soon after the founding of the state of Israel, Jewish leaders in the city had asked the cardinal to do whatever he could to help get Israel into the United Nations, a move that seemed hopelessly blocked by a number of Near Eastern countries. The always resourceful Cardinal Spellman invited all the representatives of Latin American countries, most of which were at least nominally Catholic, to dinner. There he urged them to support Israel. Cardinal Spellman could be very persuasive when he wanted to be, and Israel found itself a member of the United Nations a few days later. As a sign of respect and appreciation, the Inner-City Scholarship Fund came into existence, and it has benefited the Catholic school system in New York ever since.

As it turned out, Cardinal O'Connor did manage to attend that last dinner. I was there as well. It was, as usual, populated basically by Catholic clergy and Jewish business leaders. The rabbi of Temple Emmanuel, New York's most famous synagogue, gave a beautiful prayer at the beginning, gently alluding to the serious illness of Cardinal O'Connor, who was sitting near him on the dais. This caused a moment of intense sadness throughout the room, for most people were well aware that Cardinal O'Connor would not be among us much longer. Yet it was a wonderful moment as well, with Catholics and Jews all in prayer together for a man who was a very good friend to them all.

The Inner-City Scholarship Dinner was one of Cardinal O'Connor's final public appearances. Shortly after this his illness confined him to his residence behind St. Patrick Cathedral. He died quietly there, as had his predecessor, Cardinal Cooke. Although these two men could not have been more dissimilar, their deaths affected New York City in exactly the same way.

The entire city went into mourning. People who had disagreed with Cardinal O'Connor on every matter possible suddenly seemed grief stricken at the loss of this popular if controversial man. His death, like that of Cardinal Terence Cooke before him, showed that New York City, a place many people think of as cold and unforgiving, has a very big heart and is quite capable of showing it.

CHAPTER TWENTY-FIVE

Dr. Alice von Hildebrand

Without a doubt one of the most interesting sketches in this book—to me at least—is the present one. Alice von Hildebrand is the widow of the renowned and respected Catholic philosopher and theologian Dietrich von Hildebrand. About her husband, Pope Benedict XVI has said that, when the intellectual history of our time is definitively written, von Hildebrand will certainly be considered "most prominent among the figures of this era."[1] I couldn't agree more with the pope.

But here we will meet Alice rather than Dietrich von Hildebrand. Her own career has involved a great deal more than being a wife: She is very definitely an impressive and accomplished woman on her own terms.

Alice Jourdain was born into a French-speaking family in Belgium in 1923. Her grandfather founded *Le Libre Belgique,* which became a very popular daily Catholic newspaper; in its heyday it was considered the most Catholic newspaper in the world. For this work Alice's grandfather was recognized by the pope himself. Obviously, Alice's lineage is an impressive one.

Alice received an excellent education in the European style. She was taught primarily by Augustinian sisters, whom Alice has told me conveyed a "superb teaching of the faith." Her education, however, was interrupted when she was in her late teens. It was 1940, and the cataclysm of World War II was well underway. That year the Nazis invaded her country, and Alice's life was changed forever.

Forced to flee the Germans, she went first to France, where she managed to secure passage on the last American ship able to depart. This nearly turned out to be a voyage into disaster rather than freedom, for a German submarine appeared. Its captain announced his intention to sink the ship in precisely one hour, making passengers scramble desperately for lifeboats. When Alice arrived at hers, she was astonished to discover that there was no room left. At that moment, she said, she felt as if she "touched eternity."[2]

By the providence of God, however, catastrophe was averted, and the ship with all its passengers was saved. Hitler himself sent a message that the ship should be spared. The United States had not yet entered the war, and apparently the Nazi leader was not eager to give the Americans any cause to do so.

Arriving without further incident in New York, Alice moved in with her uncle and aunt at the Waldorf-Astoria Hotel, which has apartments for permanent residents. Although she had not yet even mastered English, she was sent to secretarial school, something that did not greatly please her. After a while, however, Alice was permitted to take some courses in the arts and sciences at Manhattanville College, and there she found herself more in her own element.

Alice found a part-time job in the library, where one day a book fell off a cart. Picking it up, she leafed through it and discovered that it was entitled *In Defense of Purity* and had been written by Dietrich von Hildebrand, a name she had never before heard. Only a few months later, she encountered that name once again. Invited by her philosophy professor to attend a lecture at his apartment, she discovered the lecturer was the author of the book: Dietrich von Hildebrand. To this day she remembers that he spoke on "Transformation in Christ," impressing her greatly.

Soon after she graduated from Manhattanville in 1944, Alice enrolled as a graduate student at Fordham, where von Hildebrand taught, making it a point to take his courses.

When the war ended Alice's family expected her to return to Belgium and rebuild her life there. Alice, however, had other ideas. Determined to pursue her academic interests, she chose to stay in the United States. She had just received her master's degree in philosophy and was on her way to her doctorate.

The young scholar planned to support herself by teaching, but it was still the 1940s, and positions on college faculties for women were a rarity, especially in fields such as philosophy. It looked as if she would never find a position, and things were becoming a little desperate when Fr. Oesterreicher, a well-known Jewish convert, saw her work, admired it, and recommended her for a position at Hunter College, which is part of the City University of New York. Alice went there as a substitute, thinking she would be able to teach for a few weeks or months at the most. Instead she remained on the faculty for nearly four decades.

Dr. von Hildebrand soon discovered herself to be somewhat unusual among philosophers and university professors, primarily because she never deviated from teaching the objectivity of truth. This may seem innocent enough, but as the years passed, it became clear that such teaching was considered dangerous heresy in the world of the university, where all things were becoming increasingly relative. Alice indicates that many on the faculty around her seemed allergic to the word *truth*, and she was not infrequently accused of teaching Catholicism rather than philosophy.

If you've ever met Alice (or Lily, as all her friends call her), you know that she would wear such an accusation as a badge of honor, and so she did for years. Her classes were filled to overflowing with eager students, despite the attitudes of other members of the faculty. If anything, rejection by so many of her fellow scholars only spurred her on to be even truer to her convictions. It became clear over time that many students welcomed her teachings on truth, finding in them the stability and sense that so much of their formal education seemed to lack.

It's not a great exaggeration to say that Alice suffered for years in the academic world. She was regularly given evening courses instead of more desirable daytime ones; she was often passed over for promotions; and she was denied tenure long after she should have received it. None of this deflected her; none of it stopped her from teaching those things she knew to be of real importance. Although some of her fellow faculty members warned students to avoid her classes, she continued to attract students in droves, and several of the non-Catholics among them entered the Church as a direct result of her influence.

In this manner, slighted by the faculty but adored by her students, Alice carried on for years at Hunter. Then in the 1980s a new president of the college instituted an annual award to the professor who received the highest student evaluation. To the chagrin of much of the faculty, Alice received this award in 1984. Right after this she retired.

Alice's teaching was inspired by her husband and his profound understanding of Catholic thought, and it was always sound, powerful teaching reflecting the objectivity of truth, which leads to the One who is the complete truth. To Alice the truth is the bond between human beings. Relativism is the seed of division.

Dr. von Hildebrand is a busy and accomplished author, having written or edited some seven books, including *The Soul of a Lion*, the definitive biography of her husband, and *The Privilege of Being a Woman*, a work that has added both sanity and sanctity to the debates on gender issues that are so characteristic of our time. As I write these words, Alice's eighty-seventh birthday is only one day away. Yet at a time of life when most people are leading tranquil and easy lives, she is as busy and as committed to the truth as ever. Her newest book, *Man and Woman: A Divine Invention*, will soon appear. I have read it and can say that it is a fine work.

Dr. Alice von Hildebrand still lectures from time to time and is very much a vital part of the Catholic intellectual scene. She seemed to me an extraordinary woman when I met her. I believe she is even more so these many years later.

CHAPTER TWENTY-SIX

Fr. Michael Scanlan

I've always been proud to call Fr. Michael Scanlan a friend, and I'm just as proud that he is a fellow Franciscan. He is, in fact, someone I've admired for many years. He's among those priests we call truly remarkable, a man of multiple dimensions and several careers. Not many men can claim to be a priest, a lawyer, and a university president. Fr. Michael has worn all those hats and, what's more, he's been a success in each of them.

If you look at his early life, however, you might be a little surprised that Michael Scanlan became a priest. It's not that he didn't come from a devout Catholic family—he did—but he took a rather circuitous route to the priesthood, starting with undergraduate work at the very prestigious Williams College in Massachusetts, a secular school. From there he moved on not to a seminary but to law school at Harvard University. It was only after practicing as an attorney for a few years that the possibility of priesthood became real for him, as did the idea of entering the religious life. He abandoned what seemed to be an exceptionally promising and profitable legal career for a life of poverty, chastity, and obedience, entering the Third Order Regular of St. Francis.

Ordained in 1964 Fr. Scanlan was on the road to a remarkable life. It wasn't long before he became rector of St. Francis Seminary in Loretto, Pennsylvania, and then president of the College of Steubenville. The latter he nurtured until it became an important force in the Church in the United States. It is now known as Franciscan University, and it continues to be an excellent and deeply Catholic university.

Never one to be confined to the academic life, Fr. Scanlan has also been among the major voices in the charismatic renewal movement, which he introduced to Franciscan University. There it took root, and although it has spread to many other areas of the Church, Franciscan University has remained its center. These days the school might legitimately be called the charismatic university of the United States, although this designation might raise some eyebrows.

Fr. Michael, however, wouldn't care. I'm sure he thinks of his involvement in the charismatic movement as a work of God, one he was chosen to participate in. Besides, after going from Williams and Harvard to the charismatic movement, and from practicing attorney to spiritual leader in the Catholic Church, he's seen it all and heard it all, and he's not fazed by much.

Did I mention that Fr. Michael is also an author? He's published quite an impressive number of books over the years, all of which offer spiritual direction and encouragement in prayer and the spiritual life. I strongly recommend his writings to you and hope that if you've never done so before, you'll start to read his books.

I see Fr. Michael as a real Franciscan in many ways. He has a delightful sense of humor and a genuine experience of Franciscan humility and simplicity. He is a man's man and a friar's friar, and I could go on to say he is a university president's president. I would not hesitate to say that with his varied experience there may be no university president in the country who has covered so many different areas of work and accomplishment.

He also can see things for what they are and see the humor in things. For example, I was once in a car with him, and as we drove we were looking up a hill on which stood a moderately sized institution surrounded by high fences. It looked forbidding, certainly no place where you would want to spend any time. Fr. Michael cheerfully explained that this had been the minor seminary of the Third Order Regular Franciscans when he was a student. The days when minor seminaries flourished were long since over, and this institution had improbably become a correctional facility for the state of Pennsylvania. We started talking about our respective experiences in seminaries as we drove on, and just before the barbed-wire fences disappeared from view, he remarked, "You know, all things considered, the place didn't really have to change very much." A wry remark like this was well-appreciated by someone like myself, who had lived though such an experience in the "good old days" before the council when seminarians in religious orders lived such strict and controlled lives that we couldn't help thinking from time to time that we were prisoners.

Fr. Michael is now largely retired but still serves as chancellor of the university, where he continues to give spiritual advice and direction and participate in its very active spiritual life. He is a man who has deepened and expanded Catholic life in the United States, a man who has brought many people closer to Christ, and a man who is a true son of St. Francis.

CHAPTER TWENTY-SEVEN

Fr. Richard John Neuhaus

For more than thirty years Richard Neuhaus and I were not only friends; we were involved in many causes together. I first met him long ago when he was pastor of a large old Lutheran church in Brooklyn. That was during the heyday of the civil rights movement, and we were both trying, in our own ways, to show the Christian dimension of that great struggle in our country.

I remember Richard's church at the time as being something of an antique. Although it was in a rather poor area of town, you could see right away that it had once been an elegant place, a house of worship for people of means. Time and demographics had changed things greatly, however, and Richard was pastor to an entirely black and quite poor congregation. He couldn't have been happier.

He was one of a large number of Protestant clergy whom I encountered during that period. Almost all of them were fine people and fine Christians. Richard was both of those things, yet I sensed early on that he was more. Although it was not quite apparent in the early years, it became very clear as time went on that in many ways Richard's sensibility was at least as Catholic as it was Protestant. As the years passed I realized he was clearly becoming more and more Catholic in his thinking. As he said years later about his conversion, it was a matter of facing the fact that he was a Catholic already.

The years went on, the struggles changed, and Richard continued to change as well—to become more and more what he really was. Finally he confronted what must have been a momentous choice. True to form, he did not shirk it; he did not delay. He requested to be received into the Catholic Church.

Each year the Church receives many converts. Few of them, however, are quite like Richard, who entered the Church as a fully formed and mature Catholic. But now there was another hurdle. He had lived his entire adult life as a member of the clergy and wished, of course, to continue this, firm in his belief that he was called to the Catholic priesthood.

Cardinal O'Connor arranged a meeting of about twenty priests, all of whom knew Richard well, and I was among them. His Eminence asked us if we thought that Richard could be ordained a priest without first attending the seminary. He was so well educated in Catholic theology, and his spirituality was so profoundly Catholic, that seminary education for him seemed somehow superfluous. The meeting didn't last very long. We unanimously agreed that his ordination was not only possible but desirable.

Shortly after this I had the marvelous experience of attending Richard's ordination. It was a beautiful event in many ways, and it was especially significant, I think, that a number of Lutheran clergy attended. None of them expressed any disapproval at all, although I'm sure they must have been disappointed to lose such a valuable member of their ranks. I must say they took it very well.

Richard was never one to waste time, and he very quickly moved into the publication of *First Things*, the magazine he edited so brilliantly for the rest of his life, as well as the establishment of the Institute on Religion and Public Life, the organization that stands behind the magazine. From the beginning *First Things* explored the important issues of our times from a religious point of view. It quickly became a venue for thinkers of various religious persuasions to debate important ideas in a culture that all too often wants to stifle the religious voice. I have had a subscription from the date of its very first publication, and I read every issue without fail.

I have also written an article for the magazine. It is interesting to note that I sometimes find myself a bit more to the liberal side than many of the current writers. I suspect that at times Richard did too. After all, I think we are both ex-members of the Democratic Party—a party that sadly no longer bears any real resemblance to the party of my youth.

Richard was a delightful, intelligent, friendly man who always had time for people who were neither sophisticated nor well-known. In his later years he could often be seen on television; he was a man whose opinions and ideas were sought after and considered. But I think it is truthful to say that at heart he never quite stopped being pastor of that poor black church in the inner city.

Richard and I experienced life-threatening illnesses at more or less the same time. He underwent treatment for a very serious malignant tumor, and I was hit by a car and left without any vital signs for nearly half an hour. We both have written extensively over the years, and so perhaps it is only natural that we each dealt with these problems in books. His was called *As I Lay Dying,* and I wrote *There Are No Accidents.*

We had all hoped and prayed that Richard's cancer was vanquished, and for a long time it seemed that it was, but cancer is a notoriously stubborn problem, and after several years it did return. Hearing this caused me great sorrow, and I made a point of seeing him whenever it was possible to do so. The last time I spoke with him is a moment I will always remember.

I was coming down the steps of the sacristy in St. Patrick Cathedral after the funeral Mass for Cardinal Avery Dulles. There was Richard, sitting comfortably in an armchair. "Richard," I said, "it's so good to see you. How are you doing?"

Of course he knew exactly what I was really asking. He looked me straight in the eye and said, in a line that could have come from one of his articles in *First Things*, "Benedict, you and I have died once already. We're not afraid of it the second time around." We both got a good laugh out of that.

It was only a few weeks later that I concelebrated Richard's funeral Mass in the Church of the Immaculate Conception on Fourteenth Street in Manhattan, a church with which he had been associated for years. It was a moving funeral, and friends from many backgrounds and many different periods of Richard's life took part in it.

Although Richard came from a rural area in Canada, he was at heart a New Yorker, and he fit perfectly into this vast, difficult, daunting place, which welcomes and challenges people from everywhere and every background. I believe he was completely at home in New York—more at home, in fact, than many who were born here. He loved the city's tempo and energy, and in some ways it matched his own.

His path from Canada to New York can be compared with his path from Lutheranism to Catholicism. As he was at home in his adopted city, he was always very much at home as a Catholic, and his robust presence certainly enriched the

Church. Perhaps it was only natural that Richard would quickly become a significant force in the Catholic Church. It is my opinion that he will be remembered as such, for he contributed greatly to the rebuilding of the Church at the end of the twentieth century and the beginning of the new millennium.

CHAPTER TWENTY-EIGHT

Cardinal Avery Dulles

No one can deny that Cardinal Avery Dulles was impressive. Ranked among the outstanding Catholic theologians of the United States to emerge after the Second Vatican Council, he possessed a powerful and incisive mind.

The son of John Foster Dulles, secretary of state under President Eisenhower, Avery grew up in a world in which frequent contact with influential political leaders was commonplace. His family was nominally Presbyterian; yet by the time Avery entered Harvard University, he freely acknowledged that faith no longer held any meaning for him, that he could not bring himself to believe that God was real. However, the life of this avowed young atheist was soon to be marked by an extreme reversal, one that would take him into the Catholic Church, the priesthood, and the Society of Jesus and would culminate with his becoming the only American theologian ever to be made a cardinal.

In his autobiographical book *A Testimonial to Grace*, which was published in 1952, Avery Dulles tells of a walk he took on a very rainy spring day. As he walked, his gaze fell upon the buds of a tree that were just bursting into bloom. The sight—one he had probably encountered innumerable times before—suddenly and unaccountably took on great significance. The flowering branches became somehow revelatory for him, causing him to become aware in a new way of the order of the universe. This awareness led him quickly and inevitably to a sense of the providence of God.

The account of Avery Dulles's conversion—so simple yet so profound—is very similar to the one described by Brother Lawrence in his classic of Catholic spirituality, *The Practice of the Presence of God*. This type of conversion is a powerful gift from God, one that is not as rare as you might think.

Many years later Cardinal Dulles told me of the next stage in his conversion, the one that led him from a general belief in God into the Catholic Church. This, too, began with a walk. As Avery strolled through the streets of Cambridge, Massachusetts, one evening, he noticed a number of people entering a Catholic Church. It was about eight o'clock, and he wondered what they might be doing.

Following them into the church, he heard beautiful Latin hymns. As a classics scholar, he was entranced and very impressed that these ordinary, middle-class people were singing "*O Salutaris Hostia*" and "*Tantum Ergo.*" The beauty of these hymns, the quiet fervency of the parishioners, and— no doubt—the presence of Jesus in the Blessed Sacrament combined to leave a lasting impression on Avery, one that would lead to his entrance into the Church in 1940.

He became utterly Catholic, yet his Protestant background marked Avery Dulles in a very powerful and positive way. Although he had drifted far from the Presbyterian Church of his childhood, he was nonetheless very much a Yankee. He epitomized the qualities we associate with this hardworking and serious-minded group of people. Old-fashioned New England morality, modesty, and frugality were always parts of his way of life. We find in Cardinal Dulles a fascinating blend of the best of Protestantism with Catholicism.

In 2001 I was fortunate enough to attend the ceremony at which Avery Dulles was made a cardinal by Pope John Paul II.

Monsignor Andrew Cusack, a very fine priest, invited me, and I remember it well. True to his New England background, Avery looked ill at ease in his red finery and seemed to be hoping that no one would notice him. In fact, the eyes of the world were on him. Although a scholar, a teacher for many years, and a profound and perceptive theologian, Avery was unique among the men who were elevated to the college of cardinals that year: He alone was not a bishop.

As he approached the pope to receive the red biretta (which now is used in place of the large red hat that cardinals received in earlier times), Avery Dulles leaned on his cane. Already eighty years old, he was the eldest of the new cardinals. With some difficulty he knelt before the pope, who placed the biretta on his head. Immediately the hat fell off. Avery reached around, found the biretta, and replaced it on his head. It immediately fell off again. The third time was the charm: Finally the red hat remained perched on the new Jesuit cardinal's head. Thus pomp and circumstance suffered a bit, but Avery Dulles stood up, a prince of the Church nonetheless, smiling a shy New England smile.

This event remained the source of a great deal of humor for Cardinal Dulles and his friends for years to come. So did a comment he once made at St. Joseph's Seminary, that he was reluctant to become a cardinal because he didn't want to wear red socks.

My most moving recollection of this great man comes from only a few weeks before his death. He was quite elderly by then, and old age had taken its toll. He was unable to speak or even to stand, yet his mind was every bit as sharp as it always had been.

By the providence of God, Pope Benedict XVI had come to New York and was at St. Joseph's Seminary. Cardinal Dulles was there, and the Holy Father made special arrangements to speak with him. It was poignant to see Cardinal Dulles, so weakened physically yet so strong intellectually and possessed of a powerful faith, humbly encounter the successor of St. Peter.

Some months before, in April 2008, Cardinal Dulles had delivered his farewell address as a professor of theology at Fordham University. Because he was so weak, the former president of the university, Fr. Joseph O'Hare, S.J., read his address for him. I leave you some of the thoughts expressed in that address in order to sum up this remarkable Jesuit priest, this wonderfully impressive New Englander who was once a Presbyterian and then an atheist and then a prince of the Church, this man who has given so much to the Church:

> Suffering and diminishment are not the greatest of evils but are normal ingredients in life, especially in old age. They are to be expected as elements of a full human existence. Well into my ninetieth year I have been able to work productively. As I become increasingly paralyzed and unable to speak, I can identify with the many paralytics and mute persons in the Gospels, grateful for the loving and skillful care I receive and for the hope of everlasting life in Christ. If the Lord now calls me to a period of weakness, I know well that his power can be made perfect in infirmity. "Blessed be the name of the Lord."[1]

CONCLUSION

The Eternal Traveler

We all encounter fellow travelers along the road. Sometimes they accompany us for lengthy parts of our journey; sometimes it seems that they are with us for only a few brief moments. They enter our lives for good or ill and then depart again, leaving us changed in some way, be it great or small.

Here I have introduced you to a handful of those who have been part of my journey. Each was important in his or her own way; each was unique; and I have no doubts that among this group are several saints. Even though many of these fellow travelers have gone home to God long ago, their influence persists as I continue my journey along life's way. I look forward to encountering them once again in the life that infinitely transcends this one, the eternal life we have been granted through the life, death, and resurrection of Jesus Christ, the life that is the ultimate goal of all journeys.

Most of those who read this book will never have met any of the people I have chosen to write about, although I hope my reminiscences have occasionally made you feel as if you have. Each human life is different, as each journey is different, and each of us meets and is influenced by a host of different fellow travelers. But we must never forget that there is one Traveler who accompanies all of us during every moment of our lives, whether we are aware of His presence or not. Our Lord Jesus Christ, the eternal Traveler, the eternal Shepherd, guides us on our journey out of nothingness. He walks with us as we make our way through our earthly life. He is the one

Traveler who remains with us every step of the way on our journey to His Father.

"If any man would come after me, let him deny himself and take up his cross and follow me" (Mark 8:34), says our Lord. These are words we must heed as we go through life, for a life well lived is a life that is lived by these words.

We never journey to God alone. We cannot. We journey in the company of Christ, who took on human flesh and experienced the many joys and sorrows of our human life, of our earthly journey. He is the fellow Traveler of every human being who has ever lived—those who know Him well and those who live and die without ever hearing His name. Many of us who try to be His disciples have no doubt that He leads every human soul. He calls to each one of us in our individual circumstances. He calls us to His Father in eternity. For this reason Christ has said, "I, when I am lifted up from the earth, will draw all men to myself" (John 12:32).

In centuries gone by, many thought that only Christians or only specific types of Christians—Catholic, Protestant, or Orthodox—were true companions of Christ. I am grateful that in our own day this rather harsh judgment has been rejected or at least greatly softened. Missionaries who write of traditional societies with very basic and superstitious understandings of religion often say that these people show virtues such as charity. These seemingly primitive people can quickly and eagerly embrace the Christian life once they are exposed to the Church's teachings. It is through the call of Christ, the eternal Traveler, that they come to this. As Christ calls to them, He calls to every human soul.

Despite this we see in our sad world many people who seem to have lost all sense of God, who seem far away from any sign of the supernatural virtues of faith, hope, and charity. Some seem to show very little of even the natural virtues of prudence, justice, courage, and temperance or even the subdivisions of these virtues, like kindness, patience, and generosity. Yet Christ still calls to them. Perhaps He calls in a special way to you. Perhaps He calls you to become a fellow traveler for such a person, a traveler through whom His call will become audible for the first time.

Life can be daunting and difficult, and it takes effort and sensitivity to make our journey in the company of others. We must never forget for even a moment, however, that this journey has a purpose: It is the journey to holiness, the journey to God. If you thoroughly reflect on your fellow travelers, you will see that often they make the road of life easier, that they illuminate your path, that they bring joy to you during times of sadness, that from time to time their lives make audible the call of the Eternal Traveler, the call of Christ.

Part of the reason for writing this book was to suggest, dear reader, that you spend some time examining your own journey and recalling the fellow travelers you have encountered along the road of life. I believe it can be very profitable to meditate on how their presence has changed you and, perhaps, brought you a little closer to God. If you do this, I am sure you will discover that they have taught you much. You can also be sure that you have taught others a great deal along the way, whether you realize it or not.

As you consider your fellow travelers carefully, perhaps you will begin to see something special in one or two of them. Perhaps you will find a hidden saint among them. There are many quiet saints; only a few have been chosen by God for fame, but many walk the road of life in the company of the Eternal Traveler, and they walk in our company as well.

I hope I have made my readers interested in learning more about some of the fellow travelers I have written about here. Following is a list of books about some of the better known among them.

MOTHER ANGELICA

Mother Angelica: The Remarkable Story of a Nun, Her Nerve, and a Network of Miracles was written by Raymond Arroyo and published by Doubleday in 2005.

FR. SOLANUS CASEY, O.F.M. CAP.

Much information can be obtained about this holy Capuchin friar at www.solanuscasey.org., which is the website for the Fr. Solanus Guild. Available from the guild is *Meet Solanus Casey: Spiritual Counselor and Wonder Worker*, a fine book by Br. Leo Wollenweber, O.F.M. CAP., the vice postulator of the cause of canonization of Fr. Solanus, published by Servant Books in 2002. Other books are also available from this website.

JUDGE WILLIAM P. CLARK

The Judge: William P. Clark, Ronald Reagan's Top Hand, written by Patricia Clark Doerner and Paul Kengor and published by Ignatius Press in 2007, is the best source of information regarding Judge Clark.

CARDINAL TERENCE COOKE

In 1990 the Rev. Terrence Weber and I wrote *Thy Will Be Done: A Spiritual Portrait of Terence Cardinal Cooke,* which was published by Alba House. This book, as well as more information on the cardinal and on his cause of canonization, can be obtained through the Cardinal Cooke Guild, which can be reached in New York City at (212) 371-1000, extension 2740.

CARDINAL AVERY DULLES
A Testimonial to Grace: And Reflections on a Theological Journey is a beautiful memoir written by Cardinal Dulles. It was published by Sheed & Ward in 1996 and is readily available.

FR. EUGENE HAMILTON
In 1998 I wrote *A Priest Forever: The Life of Father Eugene Hamilton,* which was published by Our Sunday Visitor.

KAREN KILLILEA
The book that made Karen famous was simply entitled *Karen.* It was written by her mother and published by Buccaneer Books. It is currently out of print but readily obtainable from libraries.

FR. RICHARD JOHN NEUHAUS
As I Lay Dying: Meditations Upon Returning is the memoir by Fr. Neuhaus, which I have already mentioned. It is very moving, and I recommend it highly. It was published by Basic Books in 2002. Fr. Neuhaus was a prolific author, and many of his books are in print. While they are not autobiographical, as is *As I Lay Dying,* they do reveal the depth and breadth of his thought. They can be found easily on the Internet.

FRANK SHEED AND MAISIE WARD
Wilfrid Sheed, Frank and Maisie's son, wrote *Frank and Maisie: A Memoir with Parents,* which was published by Touchstone in 1986.

MOTHER TERESA OF CALCUTTA

A great deal has been written regarding Mother Teresa. *Mother Teresa: A Complete Authorized Biography* by Kathryn Spink, published by HarperCollins in 1997, is readily available. Mother's own deeply moving words regarding her long period of darkness are available in *Come Be My Light: The Private Writings of the Saint of Calcutta*, which was edited by Brian Kolodiejchuk and published by Doubleday in 2007.

CHAPTER ELEVEN: *Sr. Mary Joseph*

1. Julia Prodis, "Socialite Gives Away Wealth to Become Cloistered Nun," *The Seattle Times*, October 20, 1994.

CHAPTER EIGHTEEN: *Fr. Bob Stanion*

1. Benedict XVI, *Spe Salvi*, 44, www.vatican.va.

CHAPTER TWENTY: *Liberal and Conservative Together in Faith: Fr. George Barry Ford and Fr. John Anthony Hardon, S.J.*

1. John Hardon, *Spiritual Autobiography*, Hardon Archive, unpublished, p. 36.

CHAPTER TWENTY-TWO: *Judge William P. Clark*

1. Norman A. Bailey, *The Strategic Plan That Won the Cold War*, as cited in Paul Kengor and Patricia Clark Doerner, *The Judge: William P. Clark, Ronald Reagan's Top Hand* (San Francisco: Ignatius, 2007), p. 163.

2. Kengor and Doerner, cited on back cover.

CHAPTER TWENTY-THREE: *Art and Mary Wiser*

1. The full and official name is the Bruderhof Church Communities International.

CHAPTER TWENTY-FIVE: *Dr. Alice von Hildebrand*

1. Cardinal Joseph Ratzinger, foreword to Alice von Hildebrand, *Soul of a Lion: Dietrich von Hildebrand* (San Francisco: Ignatius, 2000), p. 12.

2. Private conversation with Dr. Alice von Hildebrand.

CHAPTER TWENTY-EIGHT: *Cardinal Avery Dulles*

1. Cardinal Avery Dulles, as quoted in Robert P. Inbelli, "A Visit with Avery Dulles," *Commonweal*, June 1, 2008.

ABOUT THE AUTHOR

A priest for fifty years, Father Benedict J. Groeschel, C.F.R., is one of the founding members of the Franciscan Friars of the Renewal. He is a psychologist, an internationally known speaker, and a retreat master. His numerous books include *Healing the Original Wound*, *Tears of God*, *The Virtue Driven Life*, and *After This Life*. Fr. Groeschel also hosts the weekly EWTN program *Sunday Night Live With Father Benedict Groeschel*.